GENDER
AND POWER
IN THE PLAYS OF
HAROLD PINTER

GENDER AND POWER IN THE PLAYS OF HAROLD PINTER

Victor L. Cahn

Published by
MACMILLAN PRESS LTD
Houndmills, Basingstoke, Hampshire RG21 6XS
and London
Companies and representatives
throughout the world

First edition 1994
Reprinted 1998

ISBN 0–333–61502–6 hardcover
ISBN 0–333–73383–5 paperback

A catalogue record for this book is available
from the British Library.

This book is printed on paper suitable for recycling and
made from fully managed and sustained forest sources.

Printed and bound in Great Britain by
Antony Rowe Ltd, Chippenham and Eastbourne

Design: Acme Art, Inc., New York

CONTENTS

To my mother,
Evelyn Baum Cahn

ACKNOWLEDGMENTS

To Laura Heymann, of St. Martin's, for her energy, efficiency, and superb editorial suggestions.

To my brother, Dr. Steven M. Cahn, for contributions that, as ever, go beyond words.

The author wishes to thank Faber and Faber Ltd., for permission to quote from *Plays One-Four* by Harold Pinter, and Grove/Atlantic Monthly Press, for permission to quote from *Harold Pinter: Complete Works*, volumes 1-4:

All quotations from Harold Pinter's plays, unless otherwise noted, are taken from the Grove edition. Citations include volume number and page number.

Where words have been deleted from the dialogue quoted, the ellipsis is in brackets ([. . .]) to distinguish these omissions from other ellipses in the text. Quoted stage directions appear in italics.

Introduction

One of the best-known anecdotes about Harold Pinter, and one that probably better than any other reflects his relationship with the theater public, is his reply to a woman who wrote in dismay about her inability to grasp one of his plays:

> Dear Sir, I would be obliged if you would kindly explain to me the meaning of your play *The Birthday Party*. These are the points which I do not understand: 1) Who are the two men? 2) Where did Stanley come from? 3) Were they all supposed to be normal? You will appreciate that without the answers to my questions I cannot fully understand your play.

To which Pinter wrote:

> Dear Madam, I would be obliged if you would kindly explain to me the meaning of your letter. These are the points which I do not understand: 1) Who are you? 2) Where do you come from? 3) Are you supposed to be normal? You will appreciate that without the answers to your questions I cannot fully understand your letter. (Quoted in Esslin, *Pinter the Playwright*, 41–42)

The response communicates a puckish wit as well as a subtle pleasure in turning aside an audience unwilling to experience art on the artist's terms.

The exchange reflects as well an essential aspect of Pinter's drama. The central theme of his work is also the dominant theme of twentieth-century art: the struggle for meaning in a fragmented, unfathomable world. Virtually all his characters are at times uncertain of whom or what they understand, of whom or what they believe, and ultimately of who or what they are: "There is the problem of the *possibility* of ever knowing the real motivation behind the actions of human beings who are complex and whose psychological make-up is contradictory and unverifiable" (Esslin, *The Theatre of the Absurd*, 243).

This condition of incertitude regarding society and self has several theatrical consequences. Pinter's characters live in perpetual suspicion, regarding both familiar figures and strangers with trepidation. His characters are also protective of what they see as their own, objects and territory over which they can assert sovereignty. These possessions may range from the trivial (the cheese roll in *The Homecoming* or the knife in *The Collection*) to the extravagant (Deeley's home in *Old Times*). Such holdings are the most defined entities in Pinter's dramatic universe and a source of stability for men and women baffled by so much else. As a result of this state of mind, his characters are forever on guard against invasion, both physical and psychological. They are always nervous that whatever few rights and possessions they claim may be snatched away, leaving them even more alienated.

These objects, however, do not exist in a vacuum. They must be placed somewhere, and that somewhere is fundamental to an individual's identity. Thus many of Pinter's characters take refuge in a room, a construction of familiar walls and furniture about which they know as much as they can know about anything and in which they feel as safe as they do anywhere. In characterizing several of Pinter's earliest plays, George Wellwarth wrote: "The conflict in Pinter's plays occurs when one of the outside forces penetrates into the room and disrupts the security of its occupants" (Wellwarth, 225). Such is the framework for many of Pinter's works.

This struggle for survival is not a declared state of war, nor is it merely a subtle, unspoken hostility. Frederick Lumley perceptively describes it as ". . . more than a theater of understatement, it is also one of irrational impulses ever present, which create an atmosphere of nervous tension" (Lumley, 270). Here is the crux of Pinter's theatricality, the source of the unique tone that has, to the playwright's annoyance and disdain, been labeled "Pinteresque."

His characters do not attack overtly, as happens in the plays of Strindberg, Albee, or Osborne. Rather, Pinter's characters proceed tenuously, creating a stage environment in which every word, every hesitation and gesture, demands attention from both actors and audience. The characters often speak minimally, amid frequent pauses, as if wary of revealing a tidbit about themselves or their background that might create a point of vulnerability. The language is therefore dominated by unanswered questions that lead to repeated questions, awkward pauses, silences, and repetitions. To further shelter themselves, the characters rely on colloquialisms, professional jargon, and convoluted word patterns. The result is dialogue that often lacks the coherence and logic of traditional stage language but that in its disjunction reflects the mind and emotions of the speaker.

Yet despite its seeming incoherence, the speech is both familiar and realistic, as Wellwarth notes: "The dialogue in Pinter's plays fascinates by its very monotony and repetitiousness because the audience *recognizes* it—they have heard this sort of talk before" (Wellwarth, 224–225). This realism, though, is part of a unique overall effect that F. J. Bernhard calls an "essentially suprarealistic quality. Any single line of dialogue might be taken as realistic prose. But in the pattern of the play as a whole, the words have a consistent rhythmic construction and a symbolic charge that lift them beyond conventional realism" (Bernhard, 191).

Furthermore, when characters do try to explain themselves, they often do so obliquely, in seemingly random remarks or obtuse stories that appear tangential. Yet such detail, whether genuine disclosure or intentional deception, proves revelatory. As Hugh Nelson notes: ". . . it often does not matter whether what they say is, in fact, true. An invented past can be as telling as a true one" (Nelson, 151). Nonetheless, we as audience try first to ascertain to what extent the characters are speaking what they know to be truth and, second, to understand the motivations and background that lead characters to speak and act as they do. Frequently, though, we are at a loss. The details simply are not there. Clarification is not provided. In Pinter's own words, "The desire for verification on the part of all of us, with regard to our own experience and the experience of others, is understandable but cannot always be satisfied" (Pinter, "Writing for the Theatre," 11). Thus a sense of mystery pervades every play: "The audience is left to supply whatever conceptual framework it can, but no single rational frame will answer all questions . . . The plays—as aesthetic entities—are completed, but the conceptual matrices out of which the action arises are left gaping" (Schechner, 177).

Even when characters do try to divulge part of themselves, they may be unwilling or unable to speak honestly: "Words thus become barriers between the very persons they are meant to join together. They stand between persons and become part of the hard, disarranged furniture making our passage through the world more difficult" (Killinger, 102). This uncertainty of meaning, complicated by resultant multiple levels and meanings of text and subtext, is the fabric of Pinter's drama. The playwright, too, has commented that speech has ulterior motivations: "When true silence falls, we are still left with echo, but are nearer nakedness. One way of looking at speech is to say that it is a constant stratagem to cover nakedness" (Pinter, "Writing for the Theatre," 15). Consequently, the more words his characters utter, the more likely their insecurity. Yet no matter how much they talk, no matter how much they attempt to establish a bond through language, these characters remain trapped in loneliness: "Isolation is the common fate of Pinter characters; it is part of the insecurity of their world that they should be alone" (Sykes, 79).

The meticulous use of language is reflected in the physical behavior of the characters, who tend to move about the stage slowly, resorting to physical action only in desperation or after reflection and preparation. This disparity between the characters' plight and their inability or unwillingness to confront the opposition head-on contributes to the unique theatrical atmosphere that has been called "comedy of menace," a term first applied to Pinter by theater critic Irving Wardle.

The humor also grows out of a spirit of play that pervades Pinter's works. Many of his characters disguise movements under the mask of a game. In some cases the game is literal: a squash match in *Betrayal* or the football game described in *A Night Out*. More often the game is figurative: characters may relate narratives or remember incidents that become weapons. Sometimes the characters create stories that are used to establish dominance; therefore the audience, like other characters or the speakers themselves, cannot be sure where reality begins and fantasy takes over. Some games take the form of social maneuvering, as characters choose allies and enemies as a way to stake out territory. Some games are linguistic, as one character tries to outdo another with wordplay. Whatever the rules, "the game, essentially, is the continual battle for emotional security" (Gale, *Butter's Going Up,* 149).

This battle is, at its core, a struggle for power, power that in and of itself provides some verification. In a world where meaning is uncertain, where objects and territory are all that are definable, where language is a vehicle for protection rather than communication, where doubt in many forms is ever present, supremacy over other people guarantees a measure of knowledge and identity. When characters are secure in their authority, when they control others, when they are confident that their own status is certain, then they are spared some of the anguish intrinsic to Pinter's dramatic world.

What I hope to demonstrate is that in these works such conflict takes place on two planes: the conscious and the unconscious. On the conscious plane the characters are in visible conflict for territory and for power within that territory. Wardle has written that this view is the key to understanding Pinter's most famous and controversial work, *The Homecoming,* and suggests that this perspective may be applied to other Pinter plays:

> The Pinter character . . . is there to defend his room. If anyone invades it he is on his defenses; the intruder may be a victim, an ally, or an assailant. Until the proprietor finds out which, there is talk, a verbal tournament to decide who will gain the dominant position and territorial rights.   (Wardle, 38)

Pinter's characters are aware of their mutual contention, and if offensive and defensive tactics are oblique, they are nonetheless apparent to both the combatants and the audience. The second plane of conflict, however, is hidden; it is one in which characters function instinctively, propelled by biological forces of which they may not be aware. Pinter himself has suggested this very point, that his characters do not act "arbitrarily, but for very deep-seated reasons" (quoted in Hewes, 56). He was speaking about *The Homecoming,* but his words could be applied to any number of his works. Patrick Roberts has written that Pinter's "interest in people is very much at the level of the basic primitive stuff that he sees as the deepest stratum, enigmatic and threatening, of our lives . . ." (Roberts, 69). To an extent Pinter's characters operate by what playwright/anthropologist Robert Ardrey designated "the territorial imperative" (Ardrey, 7), a primal drive for possession and, thereafter, power. Peter Hall suggests a similar theatrical world when he discusses directing Pinter's plays: "My vocabulary is all the time about hostility and battles and weaponry, but that is the way Pinter's characters operate, as if they were all stalking round a jungle, trying to kill each other, but trying to disguise from one another the fact that they are bent on murder" (Hall, 22).

Within this overall framework the tone of Pinter's plays has shifted over the course of his career. In his earliest works characters are preoccupied with immediate threats and desires, and tend to be inarticulate, to use almost antipoetic language. In his later plays many characters are more concerned with the past as a force continually shaping the present, as well as with recognition of loss and age. Such figures are often sophisticated and speak lyrically and elegiacally. Yet throughout the works we feel the inevitable struggle of all these characters to find security and identity, to satisfy those instinctive needs of human nature.

The participants in this warfare vary. Several of Pinter's early plays, such as *The Room* and *The Birthday Party*, are set in lower-class environments, while most of the later ones, such as *Old Times* and *Betrayal*, take place against wealthy backgrounds. In six of his plays, including *No Man's Land*, *The Caretaker*, and *The Dumb Waiter*, female characters are absent. In works such as *The Room* and *The Birthday Party*, women play integral parts, but the focus is not on relationships between men and women.

In many of Pinter's plays, however, the key struggle for power is between male and female, and this aspect of his output is my priority. To be sure, critics have disparaged Pinter's portraits of women. One representative view is articulated by Alrene Sykes: "Does Pinter say anything more about women than that they are mothers, wives, and whores? Not, I think, a great deal" (Sykes, 106). She adds, however, that some of these women characters "are saved by their mystery and by a charging vitality that comes to life in production better than on the printed page" (Sykes, 106).

Thus Sykes acknowledges the theatricality of Pinter's world, but she does not bring out its multitude of dimension nor the numerous subtleties of mind and emotion that characterize Pinter's female characters. Moreover, when men and women in Pinter's plays compete against one another, their conflicts not only are marked by all the elements noted above, but also are exacerbated by, among other forces, sexual desire, repulsion, and jealousy. These emotions may bewilder or torment the characters themselves, whose doubts about what lies around them are made more painful by the uncertainty of what lies within them.

Furthermore, male-female conflicts take place largely apart from political or economic territory. The battlefield is the home, the most intimate arena of life. In this competition the women have some of the same goals as the men: power and security. Pinter's women do not retreat behind traditional womanly tasks. Indeed, few of these plays involve complications created by the presence of young children, and most offspring who are part of the characters' lives remain in the background. Maternal responsibility does not supplant the primary struggle for survival and authority, as the women seem determined to avoid letting gender limit their territorial rights.

Another intriguing aspect of the struggle between men and women is that the element of mystery troubles Pinter's male characters far more than it does his female characters. Many of the women in these plays operate with an understanding of their own bodies and minds and therefore of their own desires. The women also have insight into male behavior and thought. Pinter's men, on the other hand, are constantly perplexed by what women know and, even more, by what women want. Thus the overall comic tension is increased by the male realization that although men have the physical capacity to exert dominance, they are emotionally weaker than the women with whom they are in conflict.

At the same time, the dramatic tension grows because although the women may be internally more powerful than the men around them, the surrounding environment usually demands that the primary role of women is to react both to men and to predominantly male social values. In addition, even if the women in Pinter's plays do not allow maternal or domestic concerns to take over their lives, these priorities are still endemic to them. Pinter repeatedly dramatizes the psychological and physiological weapons that are unique to women and that they use in their struggle for identity and security. He implies as well that the sensibilities and more subtle needs of women are divergent from those of men. This area of distinction is especially important, for women in Pinter's works are forced to seek from men the emotional sustenance that men are often unable to provide.

Biology, mystery, passion, power: such are the components of sexual conflict in Pinter's plays.

The claim that male-female conflict is dramatized by Pinter as instinctive has been opposed by several feminist critics, who see such tensions as social constructs. One view has been offered about the characters in *The Homecoming*: "Again, the suggestion seems to be that the gender roles ascribed in language are not natural or essential or biological ones, but are instead constructed" (Sarbin, 36). Such an estimation is not a fair reading of either *The Homecoming* or the rest of the plays. To the contrary, Pinter implies that much of the behavior of men and women is the product of their nature. In his plays, social and linguistic manifestations are not causes of the roles the characters play, but products.

Another feminist perspective is offered by Elizabeth Sakellaridou in her book *Pinter's Female Portraits*, in which she suggests that his works reflect a progression in his view of women: "This initial biased sexist attitude follows a steady, though often uneven, evolution, until it eventually crystallizes into a gentler, totally, androgynous vision" (Sakellaridou, 11). This judgment may be inspired more by ideology than accuracy. Although some of Sakellaridou's insights are useful, too often she slants her readings so that they conform to her claims about androgyny, even though the plays themselves communicate a different attitude. Pinter always dramatizes men and women as fundamentally contrasting in nature, with distinct values and desires revealed in the seemingly eternal struggle for power.

Some critics resist any kind of realistic approach to Pinter's characters. In a statement that represents the post-structuralist view, Almansi and Henderson derogate audiences who react to the plays as realistic pieces: "To search for psychological plausibility, behavioural congruity, confessional eloquence or epistemological clarification in his plays is, most of the time, a vain enterprise" (Almansi and Henderson, 23). However, they also suggest that "as with Chekhov, one has to reach into the subtext of the unspoken, for rarely is there the comfort of a stated unequivocal fact" (Almansi and Henderson, 28–29). In following this second approach they end up working against their own dictum about psychological consistency, for throughout their book they grapple with the motivations and implications of characters' actions and words.

This apparent contradiction in discussing Pinter's works plagues readers who seek to avoid analyzing the plays in the context of "real life." Yet the need to find a "through line," some consistent psychological path that may be used by actors and directors to create a unified character on stage, still stands before those who would come to grips with any play. John Russell Brown helps resolve this difficulty by noting that Pinter's characters ". . . belong in the theatre only, in the exploratory world where they have their only substantial existence. One cannot imagine them in relation to other characters or in other settings; and they have no activity which is not precisely necessary to the drama" (Brown, 32). To see consistency within the confines and the rules of that world is legitimate and worthwhile:

> . . . the end result of the actions in a Pinter play may appear to be absurd, but a careful tracing of the movement of the play will prove a steady line of cause and effect, as each event is determined by the nature of the characters participating and the situation which immediately preceded it. And whatever transpires prepares for future events.   (Gale, *Butter's Going Up*, 253)

Whether any conclusions that emerge from such analyses may be applied to our own lives, however, is another question entirely:

> None of his plays, while we are actually watching them, engage us in any "issue," moral or otherwise—the "experience" given us with dramatic subtlety, verbal sophistication and a complete awareness of theatrical possibility is too strong to allow us to engage ourselves with anything else.   (Evans, 176)

This statement, though largely correct, must be modified with regard to Pinter's most recent plays, including *Mountain Language* and *Party Time*, in which overtly political themes are apparent. Otherwise, especially in matters of male-female relationships, Evans's judgment is helpful.

How Pinter's characters come to life onstage; how their singular dramatic energy propels them; how they are theatrically unified; and, in particular, how male and female characters relate to one another and their environment in the battle for survival and power: these are the major questions to be examined in this book.

1

A Slight Ache
A Night Out
Night School

The three plays discussed in this chapter are products of the early part of Pinter's career and were originally composed for a medium other than the stage. *A Slight Ache* is almost defiantly antirealistic, while the others are perhaps the most realistic works Pinter has written. Although technically they are not among his most polished works, all three reflect aspects of the male-female contention for dominance, and issues that come to the fore more powerfully in later works may be studied in incipient form here. In addition, each play dramatizes how tensions about the question of identity are created by instincts and drives that surface from within characters despite their attempts at constraint.

A SLIGHT ACHE

... the threat may not come only from outside; it is no good simply keeping our minds closed to outside influence, for even inside there the seeds of destruction may already be planted.   (Taylor, *Anger and After*, 292)

"The seeds of destruction" of which John Russell Taylor speaks are nowhere better dramatized than, as he suggests, in *A Slight Ache*, a radio drama that was first aired in 1959, then brought to the stage in 1961. From its opening line conflict is evident. Flora inquires about her husband Edward's awareness of the condition of their garden, and from that moment on Edward is uncomfortable. Initially he merely seems unable to distinguish between "honeysuckle" and "convolvulus," but this minor lacuna actually reflects the state of his marriage. Before long we realize that he knows little about the quality and depth of his wife's more personal concerns, and this ignorance makes Edward both defensive and vulnerable. First he tries to evade responsibility: "I don't see why I should be expected to distinguish between these plants. It's not my job" (*A Slight Ache*, I, 170). But Flora does not let him off the hook: "You know perfectly well what grows in your garden" (I, 170). To which Edward replies: "Quite the contrary. It is clear that I don't" (I, 170). His bewilderment about exotically named flowers mirrors his lack of understanding of his wife, a parallel emphasized by the name "Flora." Furthermore, she suggests putting up a canopy to shield Edward from the sun (I, 170), emphasizing his resistance to nature. Edward prefers the security of his house, almost as protection against potential invasion.

The structure of the play is thus established at the outset. Flora continues to challenge Edward's fitness as her husband, while he defends himself and what he believes is his rightful place. Because Edward is excluded from Flora's bond with her garden and, by implication, with the natural world, he tries to demonstrate his aggression and masculinity by destroying the wasp. He sadistically traps it in the marmalade, a comic cruelty intended to trample on her feelings, for even though she fears the wasp, she is shocked by Edward's callousness: "What a horrible death" (I, 172). Thus she reaffirms her bond with natural phenomena, and her sympathy implies that Edward is unable to appreciate her refinement. His own gesture is futile, however, for even as she grows uncomfortable with the wasp's dilemma, Edward's eyes begin to ache, a manifestation of psychological pain and emotional vulnerability. Simultaneously the wasp continues to fight for survival, inspiring more violence from Edward: "Bring it out on the spoon and squash it on a plate" (I, 173). Then he asks for the hot water to scald the creature. Eventually he crushes it, horrifying Flora: "What an awful experience" (I, 174). The bizarre nature of the execution, especially in light of the incongruous juxtaposition of her passion, his ruthlessness, and the triviality of the wasp, creates a dark laughter that pervades the play.

Momentarily Edward luxuriates in his capacity for destruction: "Ah, it's a good day. I feel it in my bones. In my muscles. I think I'll stretch my legs for a minute" (I, 174). His contentment is cut short by the entrance of the matchseller, an enigmatic and, for Edward, tormenting figure: "Why? What is he doing there?" (I, 175). Although Flora, too, lacks specific knowledge of the man's purpose, she is unshaken: "But he's never disturbed you, has he?" (I, 175). The implication is that as a woman Flora is sufficiently secure in her knowledge and understanding of herself that an intruding male presence does not throw off her equilibrium. Moreover, she is intrigued by a new masculine element in the environment. Edward, however, as a man and almost by definition insecure, finds the enigmatic intrusion a source of worry: "For two months he's been standing on that spot, do you realize that? Two months. I haven't been able to step outside the back gate" (I, 175). He seems paralyzed with fear: "It's my own house, isn't it? It's my gate?" (I, 176). He tries to find support in his largest possession. Why is Flora so serene? "He's a quiet, harmless old man, going about his business. He's quite harmless" (I, 176). The rest of the play partially resolves this question.

The object of contention, the matchseller, reminds us of the disparity between the dramatic forms of radio and stage. On radio, a character who never speaks cannot make his presence felt, and we are ultimately left to question whether he exists at all. Here we would wonder if the matchseller is the imaginary object of Edward and Flora's concern, a symbol of any object for contention. Such uncertainty would give the struggle between this couple a greater universality. On stage, however, the matchseller is tangible, a living being not quite realistic nor quite symbolic. The ambiguity is less subtle.

Edward now begins his struggle for authority, a battle with three opponents who must be subdued. One is the matchseller, whom Edward intends to keep outside the confines of the house. The second is Flora, whom Edward seeks to dominate and thereby keep as his own. The third is Edward himself, whose fears must be soothed and whose identity, through the exercise of power, must be confirmed.

Edward's first strategy is to make himself oblivious to the stranger by retreating to his work—an amorphous, impersonal essay on time and space.

This project seems the recourse of a man unable to deal with the daily challenges of life and seeking escape to less immediate questions, especially in light of Edward's dismissing Flora's inquiry about his piece on the Belgian Congo (I, 177). She, meanwhile, continues to evince an interest in the stranger: "He looks bigger. Have you been watching him? He looks . . . like a bullock" (I, 177). By so labelling him, Flora attributes to the matchseller the masculine vigor she misses in her husband. Edward, on the other hand, finds these hints disquieting, and moments later dismisses her: "Get out. Leave me alone" (I, 178). Such callous behavior is characteristic of Edward's vacuousness. The play gives us no evidence that Edward has enjoyed any success in life, and we should assume that such failure carries over to his personal life. We learn virtually nothing of friends or relationships outside his home, and the single relationship inside, that with Flora, is teetering.

Flora is briefly disturbed, but she has a curious retaliation: "O Weddie, Beddie-Weddie . . . " (I, 178). Here is the first instance in this work of one innate quality of the female as dramatized throughout Pinter's plays. She has the capacity to change roles, as Flora here suddenly shifts from wife to maternal figure. Edward's furious reaction suggests his inability to cope with such power. Almost simultaneously his eyes begin to hurt once more, another manifestation of psychological weakness that reflects Edward's impotence. Flora mocks Edward's fears: "You're frightened of a poor old man" (I, 178). The thought, repeated two lines later, suggests to us, and doubtless to Edward, that from Flora's perspective he too is old, harmless, and hence of no interest.

His first extended remarks about the matchseller are passive. Yet Edward insists that he will take action and mutters vague accusations: "The bastard isn't a matchseller at all. Curious I never realized that before. He's an imposter. I've watched him very closely" (I, 179). The lines are disconnected, the ramblings of an individual seeking to act, but unable to do so. Flora recognizes this ineptitude: "Why don't you call the police and have him removed?" (I, 179). Then she opens up a conversation with the stranger, inviting him for tea, offering to buy his matches, and, most important, welcoming him into her garden. In the context of this play, the last invitation is as personal as anything Flora could say. Here is a woman acting the sexual aggressor, while Edward returns to fume and fuss: "I know he's here. I can smell him" (I, 181). The reversal of power is one more comic element.

Edward's command for the matchseller to be brought in is a desperate attempt to meet the enemy head-on and thereby to communicate assurance. The gesture is meant as much to impress Flora as to validate Edward's self-confidence. After Flora's libidinous invitation, "I'll join you . . . later" (I, 182), Edward embarks on a lengthy monologue both comic and pathetic in its pleading. The details of the squire with the red hair and the three children are casually related, as if to communicate Edward's ease, but his need to prove his worth reappears almost at once: "I write theological and philosophical essays . . . " (I, 183). This preoccupation anticipates the philosophical writings of Teddy in *The Homecoming*, for both projects, abstract and apparently unconnected to the business of life, reflect characters who are intellectually and emotionally beaten and who try to disguise their weakness behind a mask of detachment. The insubstantiality of his assertion strikes Edward himself, who next relates details of random travel through Africa: "Most extraordinary diversity of flora and fauna" (I, 183). The reference to his wife's name is Edward's staking a claim to her, while the repetition of "fauna" in the next line suggests that he wants to move quickly from discussion of her. Edward recognizes a potential rival, and his insecurity is characteristic of several of Pinter's men. Like Teddy in *The Homecoming*, Disson in *Tea Party*, and James in *The Collection*, Edward feels that his wife's affections are tenuous, that he is only peripherally part of her life. We cannot be sure how long he has felt this way, but the presence of the matchseller has certainly brought these fears to the surface. The result is that his identity, his role in life, is equally tentative. Moreover, the implication here is that Edward's need for Flora is far greater than her need for him, another distinction between men and women that permeates Pinter's work.

In the next several lines Edward's mood fluctuates. First he brazenly changes the topic to Flora herself and describes her in flattering terms: "Charming woman, don't you think?" (I, 184), perhaps inviting the matchseller to try to take her away. At once, though, Edward retreats: "Stood by me through thick and thin, that woman" (I, 184). That most of this paean is in the past tense implies that the passion of their marriage has weakened. Nonetheless, Edward is desperate to maintain the relationship and, with that, his place in the house. Hence his challenge dissolves into a plea: "Yes, I . . . I was in much the same position myself then as you are now, you understand, struggling to make my way in the world" (I, 184). As if from embarrassment,

Edward resorts to masculine banter: "Get a good woman to stick by you. Never mind what the world says. Keep at it. Keep your shoulder to the wheel. It'll pay dividends" (I, 184). These variations in tone reflect Edward's vapidity, an insubstantiality of character and lack of certainty about who he is and what he hopes to maintain. Thus we should judge his struggle for a place in the household as an act of desperation.

When these comments earn no response, Edward's dialogue becomes even more haphazard. He runs down a list of bizarre drinks, in the hope that the barrage of odd-sounding words will overwhelm his listener. Edward invites the matchseller to remove some outer clothing, then inquires about the location of his activities. All this conviviality is preparation for the final section of the monologue, a statement of territorial claim at the heart of Edward's need: "You may think I was alarmed by the look of you. You would be quite mistaken. I was not alarmed by the look of you. I did not find you at all alarming. No, no. Nothing outside this room has ever alarmed me" (I, 187). Edward, too, is conscious of the uncertainty that lies beyond the walls of his house, and his boast unintentionally reveals that he sees the matchseller as an fearsome invader. Furthermore, instead of communicating self-confidence, the repeated denial of "alarm" has the opposite effect of implying fear.

Throughout his speech Edward's emotions range wildly. At moments he bullies; at others he whines or pleads. Never does he appear in control. Rather he seems desperate to elicit a response from the intruder; but the silence leaves Edward alone with his own thoughts and inner conflicts, and these he finds unbearable. As such he is an example of a phenomenon noted by psychologist Judith Bardwick: "The person whose sense of self is not stable nor well-defined, who has not achieved self-esteem, will fear the unknown as potentially dangerous to the self-concept he has, and he will cling to old patterns of dependence" (Bardwick, 166). Here is one more reason Edward fears leaving the confines of his house. Only when the matchseller stumbles, revealing vulnerability, does Edward express ease: "Aaah! You're sat. At last. What a relief" (I, 187).

When Flora enters, Edward tries to blunt her interest by bluffing about the previous encounter: "I should be the same, perhaps, in his place. Though, of course, I could not possibly find myself in his place" (I, 188). The first line intimates that the matchseller is no different from Edward, that Flora need not have interest in the intruder. The second line, though, suggests that the two men are indeed different, and for that reason Flora need not concern herself with the matchseller. In sum, Edward, as a man, does not know what will appeal to Flora, and in an attempt to deflect her interest, he contradicts himself.

Flora, however, is not dissuaded: "You're not still frightened of him?" (I, 189). The sentence, like the earlier belittling "Beddie-Weddie" (I, 178), reduces Edward to the level of a child, mocking his doubts even as it pretends to alleviate them. Edward's last desperate move is to attack her personally: "No, you're a woman, you know nothing" (I, 189). Edward is left muttering to himself, in Pinter's word *"hissing"* (I, 189). The action is that of a snake or other reptile, and implies that in this crisis Edward is like an animal protecting its lair. Flora's speech before she goes to the matchseller clarifies the hopelessness of Edward's position: "A woman . . . a woman will often succeed, you know, where a man must invariably fail" (I, 190). She implies that the nature of women differs fundamentally from that of men, and the subsequent monologue reinforces this interpretation.

She begins with two questions, and her solicitousness and, indeed, her gentle pace set her apart from Edward. She continues with memories, inviting the matchseller to share her experience during a flood: "The country was a lake. Everything stopped. We lived on our own preserves, drank elderberry wine, studied other cultures" (I, 190). Whereas Edward challenged the matchseller and simultaneously defended himself and his home, she is conciliatory, even solicitous.

Suddenly she moves to a more profound level of intimacy, when she recounts her rape by a poacher she thought was injured. That she chooses to reveal so much to the matchseller may seem surprising, but Flora has the self-confidence that Edward lacks and does not hesitate to reveal her deepest feelings. Furthermore, Edward has proven himself so distant a husband that Flora doubtless welcomes the opportunity to speak openly, even to a stranger. The horror of the experience she describes is undercut by her casual comment: "It was my first canter unchaperoned" (I, 191). She diminishes the brutality again when she recalls how, when serving as a justice of the peace, she acquitted that same man, who by now had grown a red beard. This narrative gives rise to all sorts of speculation. The original incident with the poacher could have been a sexual initiation, painful at the time, yet remembered with longing. The man with the beard may be the squire Edward mentioned earlier (I, 182). Did Flora marry Edward because he knew of these two incidents? Has she now grown weary of him, and does she desire someone new?

Certainly from this point on her speech and actions become more sexual. Equally interesting, however, is how they alternate between the flirtatious and the maternal while at the same time are complicated by feelings of repulsion: "God knows what you're saying at this very moment. It's quite disgusting" (I, 192). His very ugliness arouses her. In her next line, though, she reverts to seduction: "Do you know when I was a girl I loved . . . I loved . . . I simply adored. . ." (I, 192). Flora seems possessed by feelings she cannot control. She is attracted to the figure she is about to name "Barnabas"; yet she struggles to keep herself from him. Before long, though, she throws her arm around him; she kneels before him and virtually submits to him, then offers to give him a bath and put him to bed. The implication is that despite her capacity to delve into her own drives, even she does not understand the depth of her craving for affection.

When Edward momentarily intrudes, Flora rejects him subtly, inspiring the grossest insult Edward has summoned thus far: "You lying slut. Get back to your trough!" (I, 193). Edward's inability to turn his wife's interest away from the stranger manifests itself in rejection of her. Edward cannot deal with his incapacity to satisfy all Flora's needs, and thus he blames her for his failure. He is gradually losing his place, his territorial claims, and his power and identity.

In his desire to justify his attitude, and even his life and himself, Edward begins a lengthy recital. He recalls playing sports, inviting a response of manly bonhomie, but the matchseller's silence proves infuriating: "God damn it, I'm entitled to know something about you! You're in my blasted house, on my territory, drinking my wine, eating my duck!" (I, 194–195). The mixture of fury and bluster, climaxing with the ludicrous image of "eating my duck," makes Edward as ridiculous as he is helpless.

The next section is Edward's climactic attempt to deny his fears. In detail he describes the security of his room, the home he has built for himself and Flora. Although he never mentions her, the insinuations are, first, that Edward has established living space here, and, second, that he controls the territory surrounding this house. Or at least that he used to control the territory, for the narrative is largely in past tense, again implying that

Edward's authority has dwindled. The matchseller is evidently unimpressed, as Edward accuses him of laughing. Faced with scorn for the world he has created, Edward takes a desperate stab: "Why did I invite you into this room? That's your next question, isn't it? Bound to be?" (I, 196). He is never able to provoke an answer. Instead he talks circuitously, until he notices the matchseller weeping: "For me. I can't believe it. For my plight. I've been wrong" (I, 197). Edward urges him to "Pull yourself together" (I, 198), but the matchseller's illness seems to transfer to Edward, who reveals the discomfort in his eyes, then collapses on the floor. His last speech is a lengthy recital of both affirmation and denial, as Edward recalls his withstanding discomfort amid the elements. Again the matchseller laughs, and in horror Edward realizes that he himself is the object of mockery: "You look younger. You look extraordinarily . . . youthful" (I, 199). Growing weaker, he invites the matchseller to the garden, recalling himself when young: ". . . when a stripling . . . no more than a stripling . . . men twice my strength . . . when a stripling . . . like yourself " (I, 199). Burkman suggests that such revelation echoes the plight of a figure from classic myth: "Like Oedipus, who blinds himself when he achieves insight, Edward's diminishing sight, the slight ache in his eyes, seems to take place as he suffers new insight into himself and his situation" (Burkman, "Death and the Double," 136).

While Edward's masculinity fades in the presence of a rival, Flora is inspired by a new man who rekindles her passion and love. She embraces the matchseller, to whom she opens her garden and her home: "Take my hand" (I, 200). The image is both romantic and maternal, and corresponds to Flora's complex attitude throughout the play. She also refers to him as "Barnabas" (I, 200), which, as Burkman has pointed out, means "summer" (Burkman, "Death and The Double," 137). In a footnote Burkman elaborates: "The day of Saint Barnabas, June eleventh in the old style calendar, was the day of the summer solstice, and Barnaby-bright is the name for the longest day and the shortest night of the year" (Burkman, "Death and the Double," 144). Such overtones reinforce that in contrast to Edward, a figure of lifelessness, the matchseller, though dark and dirty, nonetheless embodies a renewal of love and life for Flora. Burkman also suggests about Pinter: "Even though he explores his theme in the context of a seasonal fertility ritual, [his] subject is a crisis of identity, his theme, the alienation of modern man" (Burkman, "*A Slight Ache* as Ritual," 334). Sakellaridou agrees: ". . . the way the play traces

Edward's gradual decline and pursues his downfall makes it clear that this man is a helpless creature who does not know even his own identity. Edward definitely bears the germ of his destruction in himself " (Sakellaridou, 82).

Flora's last act is to give Edward the matchseller's tray. She has no more use for him, although perhaps it would be more correct to say that he can be of no more use to her. Thus *A Slight Ache* dramatizes male fear, what throughout Pinter's work is portrayed as a primal male anxiety of rejection by a female whose need and capacity for emotional and physical love are beyond his capabilities. The play also emphasizes that Edward's failure reflects loss of place and identity.

Most important, however, is the instinctive tension between male and female identity. While Edward has aged and grown more fearful, he has also become more selfish, retreating behind pointless preoccupations and denying Flora the emotional sustenance she desires. The matchseller, though passive and silent, does not turn away, and for Flora such behavior is an offer of acceptance. Her eagerness to bring him into her life and to share her garden and home suggests that in spite of age she retains a spiritual and emotional vitality that contrasts starkly with Edward's inevitable diminution of masculine power. This theme recurs throughout Pinter's plays, as female emotional energy often challenges male physicality in a struggle for power and identity.

A NIGHT OUT

A Night Out, originally presented on television in 1960, premiered almost simultaneously with the release of Alfred Hitchcock's *Psycho*. Given that proximity, Pinter could not have been influenced by the movie. Yet the two works share the theme of a dominating mother whose love is all-encompassing. In *Psycho* that love survives even the mother's death, ultimately usurping, then destroying, Norman Bates's personality. The situation in this play is not so extreme, but Mrs. Stokes's feelings for her son clearly go beyond the maternal.

Furthermore, the intermingling of maternal affection and sexual desire that is at the heart of *A Slight Ache* is also dramatized in *A Night Out*. From the first scene Albert Stokes is dominated by his mother, and even as he plans his evening at a party given by a business associate, she expresses so much doubt and fear that Albert is forced to comfort her: "I won't be late. I don't want to go. I'd much rather stay with you" (*A Night Out*, I, 206). During the rest of the scene she continues to stifle him: "You're all I've got, Albert. I want you to remember that. I haven't got anyone else. I want you . . . I want you to bear that in mind" (I, 206). A few lines later she warns: "You're not messing about with girls, are you? You're not going to go messing about with girls tonight?" (I, 207). Throughout the play Albert struggles to establish power and a sense of self by the assertion of masculine prerogatives.

What is not evident is whether Mrs. Stokes is aware of either the depth of her attachment or how her possessive devotion has perverted Albert's life. Every few lines Mrs. Stokes mentions her dead husband, and therefore we feel that she both wants and needs her son to take his father's place. Yet at the start Pinter does not portray Mrs. Stokes as evil or as consciously throttling Albert. Rather, she is desperate for love, and her son is the only possible source. Hence she may be regarded as the victim of instinctual needs. However, her constant references to her dead husband, implying that somehow he would be hurt by any neglect Albert showed toward his mother, hint at a more monstrous side that becomes apparent later.

Albert, too, has such drives, although they do not disclose themselves immediately. At the start he is polite, even obsequious, to his mother, although his leaving for the party is an act of rebellion. The climactic moment of the first scene is when she touches her breast, claiming that there is where his father still lives (I, 207). The gesture reveals her moving desperation, but the simultaneous sexual overtones are painful.

We learn about some of Albert's personality through the discussion about his participation in a football match. He does have latent aggression, for he was able to compete effectively on the pitch, although his last game was not a strong effort, as he was deceived by a faster player (I, 211). This report is contrasted sharply by the next scene, in which Mrs. Stokes fusses over Albert's clothing, reminding him that his father "always looked liked a gentleman" (I, 213). More than ever we feel her literally grooming her son to take her husband's place, and what earlier looked like kindness is turning more insidious. In scene 4 the potential violence in Albert appears again, when in response to questions about his mother he grows testy: "What are you getting at?" (I, 217). Again, not all this anger is rational. Instead Pinter dramatizes Albert as possessing, or possessed by, forces seething inside him, and the primary tension of the play is anticipating how this anger will be released. Further strain is injected by Kedge's remarks about his own mother: "Mine's fine too, you know. Great. Absolutely great. A marvel for her age, my mother is. Of course, she had me very late" (I, 217). He glosses over the subject, as if unwilling to acknowledge any strain in the relationship, but we assume that the comment gnaws at Albert, who cannot be so dismissive.

Albert's inability to mix in a normal social setting is dramatized in the first scene of act 2, where amid flirting and dancing he is alienated. We feel this estrangement particularly when Eileen and Joyce sit on either side of him (I, 223–224). Albert can barely acknowledge their coquettish jibes, and when they mention his mother he walks away. His incipient violence moves closer.

When Eileen shouts in dismay about being touched, and suspicion is falsely cast on Albert, rebellion begins. He fights back verbally when Gidney calls him by his first name, as Albert's mother might do. Then when Gidney openly labels Albert "a mother's boy" (I, 230), Albert's retaliation is his initial physical response. The implication is that Albert's sexual frustration is emerging in violence, and the rest of the play dramatizes that the two forces—sex and violence—that reflect Albert's need for self-assertion also are inextricably linked as part of human nature.

Both themes are reaffirmed in the next scene, when Albert's mother offers a monologue that intensifies her dominance as well as her desperation:

> I wouldn't mind if you found a really nice girl and brought her home and introduced her to your mother, brought her home for dinner, I'd know you were sincere, if she was a really nice girl, she'd be like a daughter to me. But you've never brought a girl home here in your life. I suppose you're ashamed of your mother.   (I, 232)

We sense that her claims are fraudulent, that she is actually inviting Albert to reply that because he has her, he needs no one else. He, however, says nothing, and in response she becomes more extreme:

> But one thing hurts me, Albert, and I'll tell you what it is. Not for years, not for years, have you come up to me and said, Mum, I love you, like you did when you

were a little boy. You've never said it without me having to ask you. Not since
before your father died.   (I, 233)

Perhaps the responsibility of fulfilling part of his father's role was too much
for Albert, and he withdrew into himself. Now, under the pressure of verbal
torments from his colleagues, physical enticement from women, and relentless suppression by his mother, Albert cannot control his anger. His smashing
of the clock, a symbol of the past and therefore of his own entrapment, is a
breaking away from all such shackles and a statement of his own will. True,
we never see this action but only hear Albert's narrative later. Yet the threat
itself communicates his anguish.

Albert's encounter with the prostitute is especially curious in terms of this
anguish. Early on she points out a photo of her daughter, and thereafter the
maternal and the sexual are united in Albert's image of her. She takes offense
when he curses under his breath, and her chastisement sounds like something
Mrs. Stokes might say: "Do you mind not saying words like that?" (I, 236).
Throughout the scene the girl, as Pinter calls her, maintains an image of
delicacy, while Albert resists taking action with her. Perhaps her comparative
elegance reminds him too much of a mother figure, and he is unable to respond.
What catches his attention first is the clock, an obvious reminder of his
mother's apartment, and that he fixates on it so quickly hints that more
violence lurks within him against this female figure. The girl cautions him to
use his handkerchief, then berates him in words that again sound like some
Mrs. Stokes might invoke: "What on earth's the matter with you? What have
you been doing tonight?" (I, 239). The girl maintains this tone when she
assaults him for dropping the cigarette on the carpet, an event that pushes
Albert over the edge. His verbal attack is ostensibly against the girl, but we
cannot miss the implication that he is talking to his mother as well: "Who do
you think you are? You talk too much, you know that. You never stop talking.
Just because you're a woman you think you can get away with it" (I, 242).
His anger resounds beyond the woman in this room: "You haven't got any
breeding. She hadn't either. And what about those girls tonight? Same kind.
And that one. I didn't touch her!" (I, 243). Esslin suggests that this outburst,
in conjunction with the rest of the scene, implies Albert's rejection of the
maternal and the sexual, "both aspects of the feminine principle" (Esslin, *Pinter
the Playwright*, 98). Albert is also rejecting his own subjugation to that

principle, as he scorns the girl for being beneath him. He takes pride as well in his refusal to be used, so to speak, by Eileen and Joyce earlier. Thus Albert communicates triumph at his resistance to biological drives and needs. He is denying not only the feminine, but also his own masculine side.

The rest of the scene confirms this perspective. He threatens to break the clock, a gesture that in his mind unites the girl with his mother. Then he is distracted by the picture of the child. Reading the inscription on the back, he decides that the subject is not the girl's daughter, but the girl herself, and he crumples the photo. When the girl moans in pain, Albert takes satisfaction in destroying her illusions of motherhood: "That's not your daughter. It's you! You're just a fake, you're just all lies!" (I, 244). We also sense that he is again attacking his own mother, vicariously breaking off her happiness. He then orders the girl to put his shoes on him and tie the laces, the sort of maternal task that Mrs. Stokes has forced upon him. Now, however, Albert is compelling a woman to act; afterward he dismisses her with insults and a contemptuous toss of a coin. The rejection is not only of the girl but of all motherly affection he has had to endure.

Will this streak of independence survive? In the final scene Albert seems at ease with himself until his mother's voice calls and *"his body freezes"* (I, 246). Thereafter he sits silently, as Mrs. Stokes admonishes him for earlier actions against her. Simultaneously she verbally strokes him, assuring both him and herself: "You're good, you're not bad, you're a good boy . . . I know you are . . . you are, aren't you?" (I, 247). She is trying to reestablish herself as the power over his life.

Thematically *A Night Out* has several important connections with *A Slight Ache*. In each play a male figure experiences a kind of impotence. Edward can neither thwart the invading presence of the matchseller, nor win back Flora, while Albert cannot deal with either his friends in business or the girl. In each play the frustrated male resorts to violence: Edward kills the wasp, while Albert threatens the women around him. In each play the dominating female switches roles. Edward's wife plays a maternal role that leaves Edward lost and helpless, while Albert's mother takes on the role of lover and embraces Albert back into the snare from which he desperately wants to escape.

We cannot be certain whether Albert's brief rebellion is the start of a complete breaking away, or whether he will return to utter submission. The implication is that his attachment to his mother, the instinctual bond between two people, as well as his need to belong somewhere and to thereby confirm his identity, is stronger than any desires for escape he may harbor. That need is one he shares with many of Pinter's male characters.

NIGHT SCHOOL

Night School, originally written for television, was first presented on stage in 1960 and then transferred to radio. Pinter, however, judged the play unsuccessful, and the script was not published until 1967, after the playwright revised it. Even in its present form the work is comparatively slight, with virtually none of the enigmatic qualities that distinguish Pinter's other plays, but it is nonetheless worth scrutiny, especially with regard to the question of the creation of identity through exertion of power.

The comedic tone is established at the outset, as Walter returns from prison to the home where he lives with his two aunts. They fuss over him maternally, alternately stuffing him with cakes and scolding him for his life as a small-time crook. The initial tension occurs with Milly's question: "Well? Have you told him?" (*Night School,* II, 202). After some byplay the aunts reveal that they have rented Walter's room to Sally Gibbs, a young schoolteacher they praise as a woman of refinement. Nonetheless, Walter is angered: "Listen, you don't understand. This is my home. I live here. I've lived in that room for years—" (II, 205). His territorial needs have been violated, for the room is the only stable element in his life; without it he is lost. Even his aunt's comforting words about Sally fail to deter Walter, who protests with comic obstinacy: "I'm used to something better. I'm used to privacy" (II, 207).

When Walter meets Sally, however, his attitude softens, and to win her affection he romanticizes his life, hinting, for instance, that he has kept a gun in the room (II, 210). In rummaging he comes across a picture of Sally, dancing in what looks like a nightclub. His curiosity is piqued by the duality between this mild schoolteacher and the racier double life she may be leading.

To learn more about her, Walter seeks the aid of Solto, the landlord and a man with all sorts of underworld contacts. Solto is a fantastic figure, who spins elaborate yarns about his own life. He is one of the first of Pinter's characters to use narrative fantasy for both self-definition and as a way to achieve superiority. As he rambles, we feel that he himself is unaware of the truth: "I was only a pubescent. I killed a man with my own hands, a six-foot-ten Lascar from Madagascar" (II, 212). Solto turns aside Walter's request for a business loan but is sufficiently intrigued by Sally's picture to conduct an inquiry: "What have you done? Fallen in love with a photo?" (II, 215). Indeed, Walter has fallen for the image of Sally.

The power of fantasy becomes more apparent in the next scene, when Walter and Sally are alone in what has become her room. Walter slips into the pose of the romantic thief, but with humorous ineffectuality. First he claims to be a gunman; then he tries to glamorize his days as a convict: "The day I left the Governor gave me a personal send-off. Saw me all the way to the gate. He told me business at the library had shot up out of all recognition since I'd been in charge" (II, 219). The story is an attempt to establish identity and, concomitantly, to win Sally by dominating her.

Walter's advances become overtly erotic. First he tries to soothe any trepidation she might have about his profession: "You don't want to worry about me being an armed robber. They call me the gentle gunman" (II, 221). Then he claims to be married to three other women: "I'm a triple bigamist" (II, 221). Yet Sally seems intrigued: "You haven't got such bad eyes yourself" (II, 222). Eventually Walter gives her orders: "Cross your legs. (*Pause.*) Uncross them. (*Pause.*)" (II, 223). Whether she conforms as he commands is unclear, but what is certain is that in Walter's mind, power and sexuality are entwined. The scene resembles Albert's episode with the prostitute in *A Night Out.* Just as Albert is stifled by his mother, so is Walter dominated by his aunts. Moreover, in both situations frustrated affection takes the form of authority that verges on the sadistic. In this scene, though, an additional struggle exists between Walter and Sally, for he cannot be sure of her identity. That uncertainty, the knowledge she holds about herself, becomes her weapon, one wielded by characters in many of Pinter's later plays.

We see another side of Sally in a later scene. Until this point she has been reactive, even meek. Now she is propositioned by Solto, who has inquired about the photo and discovered the truth about her. Here Sally proves herself independent: "I'll kick him in the middle of his paraphernalia one of these days" (II, 226). The scene is interrupted by a moment with Annie and Walter, who comment on how beautifully Sally has arranged the room. Thus the theme of reality versus appearance, the image of order versus the uncertainty behind the image, is quietly interjected (Gale, *Butter's Going Up*, 108).

The action then returns to the nightclub, where Sally increases her aura of mystery by boldly giving herself another name in front of Solto: Katina. When, however, Solto discloses that Walter has given him the picture, Sally recognizes that her double life will be exposed. We cannot be certain whether she does not want to hurt Walter, or whether she fears being revealed for what she is. Nor do we ever learn conclusively her real name or the truth about the relationship between her job as a teacher and her nightclub work. The image she maintains is the foundation of her power.

When Walter comes to Solto to find the "truth" about Sally, Solto puts him off with a bizarre denial: "There's no one to know. You've never seen her. I've never seen her. There's no one to see" (II, 232). Walter tries to find her, but she has departed, leaving only a note. The final trace of evidence is a picture of Sally among schoolgirls, holding a netball. The play ends on a poignant note, as Walter mourns what might have been a chance for love, a chance now lost.

That Walter and Sally are never able to confront each other openly about their real selves is the saddest element of the play. Other aspects, though, are also important. The Sally/Katina duality is reflected in other Pinter women who embody such contradictory instincts, such as Sarah in *The Lover*. Furthermore, Walter's desire to possess such an alluring, yet mysterious, woman reflects Stanley's desire for Lulu in *The Birthday Party*. But Sally is not as passive as Lulu. Elizabeth Sakellaridou suggests that Sally "has a firm personality and a clear identity. Psychologically she is reconciled with the idea of her dual nature" (Sakellaridou, 84). This claim is too strong, especially in the light of Sally's running away. Nonetheless, Sally does have an understanding of herself, a strength set off by Walter's weak acceptance of his inability to comprehend her nature, as reflected in his last line: "That's what it looks like" (II, 233). Walter may understand the complexities of a dual nature, but he is not strong enough to oppose it.

Perhaps most significant, the attempts by Sally, Solto, and Walter to achieve verification through narrative parallel similar efforts by a host of other Pinter characters. The authority of knowledge, in concert with the fear and tension created by uncertainty in the mind of an another, proves an overwhelming weapon in the struggle to achieve power and simultaneously to find identity and security.

THE ROOM, THE BIRTHDAY PARTY, AND THE HOTHOUSE

Some aspects of the tensions arising from the relationship between gender and power in these three plays are also found in Pinter's two earliest works, *The Room* and *The Birthday Party*. In these plays male-female conflicts are peripheral to the primary conflicts, but nonetheless deserve brief consideration.

In *The Room* (1957) Rose is trapped in a lifeless marriage, and her lengthy monologue that starts the play, addressed to an unresponsive husband, reflects a woman seeking love, but finding herself without it. This opening speech also reveals Rose's more general fears, as she ponders the identity of her neighbors: "I've never seen who it is. Who is it? Who lives down there?" (*The Room*, I, 102). She takes refuge in her room, the territory that provides some certainty against the hostility and anonymity of the world outside, but we still sense in Rose the longing that marks Flora and a host of other female characters in subsequent Pinter plays.

The other marriage in the play, that between the young couple, Mr. and Mrs. Sands, also reflects the theme of lovelessness. They bicker incessantly, and Mrs. Sands tends to treat her husband like a child, as when she orders him to sit down and warm himself, while she castigates him for other behavior (I, 112). Mr. Sands resents her attitude, but his anger also communicates a general antagonism to females that is common to many of Pinter's men: "Well, who did then? That's what I want to know. Who did? Who did bring me into the world" (I, 116). As indicated earlier, this male tendency to see the maternal and the sexual united in individual women recurs in Pinter's plays, and contributes to the failure of the male struggle for assertion, power, and identity.

The unity of the maternal and the sexual is also an important element in *The Birthday Party*. Here Meg is trapped in a lifeless marriage with Petey. Her dual instincts are apparent almost from the start, but Petey is unresponsive, and Meg thus turns her attentions to Stanley, the exotic boarder in their seaside resort. She alternately pampers and pursues him, and although she is a comic, even bizarre figure, something in her chase is sad, as when she offers him tea, then flirts pathetically: "Say sorry first" (*The Birthday Party*, 27). Moments later she strokes his arm: "Oh, Stan, that's a lovely room. I've had some lovely afternoons in that room" (I, 29). Then she tickles him, perhaps maternally or perhaps as a sexual overture. The dual possibility reflects both aspects of her.

Meg's resemblance to Flora in *A Slight Ache* goes further, for as Flora is distressed by her desires, so Meg seems almost repulsed by her own. When Stanley uses the word "succulent" (I, 27), Meg is outraged at its connotations. Yet moments later she uses the same word to entice Stanley: "Am I really succulent?" (I, 29). Again, this split sensibility, this conflict between desire and revulsion, characterizes several of the women characters to be considered subsequently.

The other female figure in *The Birthday Party* is Lulu, whose sexuality is more blatant and less complicated than Meg's. In act 1 Lulu's presence torments Stanley, who clearly desires her: "How would you like to go away with me?" (I, 36). Perhaps he hopes that domination of Lulu will give him security, but Stanley is too ineffectual to pursue her, and she dismisses him: "You're a bit of a washout, aren't you?" (I, 36). Lulu is more attracted to Goldberg, who, like Solto in *Night School*, is a gangster with a romantic surface. In act 2 Lulu sits playfully on Goldberg's lap, as he offers narratives about his wife and allows Lulu to play the role of little girl. Although through most of the play Goldberg pursues Stanley, Goldberg himself worries about his role in the nameless organization he serves, and his attachment to Lulu may be regarded as an attempt at self-definition. Like Sally in *Night School*, Lulu is largely a reactive figure. Still, just as Sally is sufficiently independent to leave Solto and head out on her own, so is Lulu assertive near the end when she accuses Goldberg: "You quenched your ugly thirst. You taught me things a girl shouldn't know before she's been married at least three times!" (I, 90). Instead of turning his aggression back at him, Lulu leaves. Perhaps this action reflects the self-reliance that also characterizes Sally. Secure in their self-knowledge, both women need not compete for dominance and identity. Several women characters in later plays of Pinter have that same security. Unlike Lulu and Sally, however, these women do not strike out on their own. They seek relationships with men and therefore become involved in the inevitable battle for territorial and personal authority.

Nonetheless, *The Birthday Party* does contain a brutal expression of that need for power, when at the end of act 2 Stanley tries to strangle Meg, then to rape Lulu. Here is a man tormented by a hostile world that has, in the form of Goldberg and McCann, denied him freedom and identity. Stanley's only recourse is the release of sexual and emotional aggression at the most assailable targets, the women around him. Stanley's attempt here is futile, but it anticipates the desperate struggles for knowledge and authority carried on by male characters in other Pinter plays in which the release of energy takes other forms, both physical and psychological.

One other female character from Pinter's early works deserves mention: Miss Cutts from *The Hothouse*, a play written in 1958 but not performed until 1980. As a figure who alternates between sexuality and authority, Miss Cutts embodies the duality intrinsic to many women in Pinter's plays. She has affairs simultaneously with Roote and Gibbs, the two men in charge of the hothouse or mental hospital, and in that role flirts boldly: "Do you think I'm feminine enough, darling? Or do you think I should be more feminine?" (*The Hothouse*, 49). She asks this question repeatedly, as if unsure of who or what she is or is supposed to be. She also takes part in the ruthless examination of Lamb, and her questions about his personal history (for example, "Have you always been virgo intacta?" [34]) become a manifestation of a social system, embodied here by a woman, intended to subdue individual identity. Sakellaridou asserts that "Miss Cutts's portrayal reflects the Freudian theory that women should find fulfillment in their own femininity and leave higher considerations to men" (Sakellaridou, 51). This claim, however, is imposed on the text. As Miss Cutts reverts from sexuality to authority, then back again, she should be seen as another victim of an oppressive system, trying to establish her place within the hierarchy of the institution and thus to achieve her own territorial control.

In the early works of Pinter discussed in this chapter, the contentions between men and women are charged by several intriguing dynamics. The male capacity for violence is counteracted by female emotional strength. The male need for authority is counteracted by the female capacity to play differing roles. The female need for emotional intimacy is set against the male need for insulation and retreat as defense against outside forces. Yet the sexes share at least one common goal: to gain control so as to establish identity and security. As Pinter's technique expands and his characters develop in a variety of ways, this competition for power between men and women remains a pervasive theme.

2

The Collection

> Our reality doesn't change: it can't change! It can't be other than what it is, because it is already fixed for ever. It's terrible. Ours is an immutable reality which should make you shudder when you approach us if you are really conscious of the fact that your reality is a mere transitory and fleeting illusion, taking this form today and that tomorrow, according to the conditions, according to your will, your sentiments, which in turn are controlled by an intellect that shows them to you today in one manner and tomorrow . . . who knows how? . . . Illusions of reality represented in this fatuous comedy of life that never end, nor can never end!
>   (Pirandello, 266)

So speaks the Father in the climactic speech of *Six Characters in Search of an Author*, in which he crystallizes the distinction between artistic figures like himself, who are, in Pirandello's words, "true" (i.e., unchanging and immortal), and human beings, who are "real" (i.e., mutable and mortal). This depiction of all human identity as relentlessly fluid and therefore beyond certainty has been compared to the world of Pinter's characters, many of whom remain amorphous and whose chameleon-like qualities are a source not only of mystery but of strength.

Pirandello also dramatized in several works the relativity of knowledge. For instance, in *It Is So (If You Think So)* Signora Frola and Ponza hold incompatible views about the identity of Ponza's wife, and the play presents the townspeople's attempts to ascertain the facts. The wife, however, refuses to clarify: "I am whom you believe me to be" (Pirandello, 138). For Pirandello absolute truth is beyond comprehension. Pinter, too, has commented upon what he sees as this aspect of the human personality:

> When an event occurs—some kind of sexual event in *The Collection*, for example—it is made up of many little events. Each person will take away and remember what is most significant to him. The more other people try to verify, the less they know.   (Quoted in Gordon, 52)

Pinter and Pirandello both seem to view human nature and knowledge as innately unknowable. Yet an important distinction must be made. In the plays of Pirandello truth is beyond confirmation. It is metaphysically uncertain. In Pinter's plays, though, truth can be revealed, but characters often withhold or ignore it to gain a psychological edge that changes perception and becomes a weapon in the struggle for power. In *The Collection*, specifically, even if the sequence of events were stated with assurance, such a revelation would neither resolve conflicts within all four characters nor permit them to reach emotional equilibrium.

Indeed, the characters who could shed light, Bill and Stella, constantly mock those who seek it, Harry and James. What gives this mockery an extra sting is that Harry and James, the economically stronger and therefore ostensibly dominant members of their respective relationships, are weakened psychologically by the desperation to know. By withholding knowledge, or by presenting it so obtusely that details blur beyond clarification, Bill and Stella retain their own, ultimately more important, strength. An additional point of interest is that a sexual power struggle occurs not only in the heterosexual relationship between Stella and James, but also in the homosexual relationship between Harry and Bill and in the less easily defined relationship between James and Bill. Thus knowledge becomes a weapon in the struggle for dominance and control, providing the victor with identity and security and leaving the vanquished with neither.

From the opening lines the script has elements of a mystery. When Harry answers the phone, the voice on the other end refuses to identify itself. From this point on, the question of identity becomes the core of the play. True, we eventually learn that James is the name of the person who makes this initial call, but his nature remains a cipher, even to James himself. In scene 2 he continues to try to exert dominance, as he refuses to answer Stella's question about whether he will be in that night (*The Collection*, II, 122). Such disregard for Stella's feelings suggests the coolness between these two and might be a reason why Stella raised the matter of possible infidelity with Bill.

The Collection was originally written as a television play, then produced on stage a year later in 1962. In the stage production the set is divided into three parts, so that Stella may remain in constant view, as Anna does in *Old Times*. The result is that even though Stella has the fewest lines, her presence communicates steadily growing power. Yet her isolation evokes our sympathy. The men have business and social contacts, but we never see Stella with anyone beside James, and her loneliness could be another reason she seeks Bill's company.

Stella's authority is contrasted with Harry's weakness, which is apparent from the stumble he takes before he speaks. Bill's scorn is also evident at once: "What have you done?" (II, 123). Harry is the older man in this relationship, and Bill depends on him for food and shelter. Harry, however, is the more insecure, because he needs Bill for emotional reasons and spends virtually all the play justifying himself to Bill and demanding that Bill be honest with him. In this respect Harry shares the plight of Edward in *A Slight Ache*, Disson in *Tea Party*, and Deeley in *Old Times*, all of whom suffer from a psychological poverty that makes them vulnerable.

The tensions between Harry and Bill are obvious in the trivial bickering over juice and toast, as well as in the more significant quarrel about each other's social habits. Although the comment is brief, Bill resents Harry's attending a party without him (II, 124), and beneath the brittle exchange lurks the implication that Bill would be unacceptable in Harry's circle. Thus when Harry probes about the mysterious phone call, then inquires whether Bill met anyone during the last week, we sense that although these two characters are bound by mutual need, they are also antagonists, for each resents that need. Bill recognizes that Harry provides financial stability, but Bill is frustrated that he requires such stability; Harry is angry that he requires

Bill for sexual and emotional sustenance. Each struggles to prove his superiority in the relationship, to diminish the importance of his own need, and to clarify the desperation of the other's:

> In the Pinter world, the exploration and confirmation of relationships is the central focus of the verbal activity of the characters. On it hinges their capacity not to achieve public goals whether social, political, or religious, but basically to confirm their estimate of their own identity and to survive.   (Quigley, 66)

The splitting of the scene between the two apartments reaffirms the solitude endured by Bill and Stella. He is left reading a magazine, while she is alone with her cat.

The most intriguing relationship in the play begins when James meets Bill. James's reason for the visit is to ascertain whether Stella has had an affair with Bill, but before long James appears to have a different concern. After the inquiry about olives, a futile attempt to make Bill uneasy, James comments on Bill's appearance: "You're not a bad-looking bloke" (II, 129). Bill answers with detached amusement: "That's more than I can say for you" (II, 129). James questions Bill about his vacation in Leeds the previous week, but the roundabout inquiry (II, 130–131) suggests that James enjoys the playful maneuvering. Finally James "*casually*" states his accusation: "My wife was there. That's where you slept with her" (II, 131). James's last name, by the way, is Horne, a word with overtones of cuckoldry.

Bill remains unperturbed: "I was nowhere near Leeds last week, old chap. Nowhere near your wife either, I'm quite sure of that. Apart from that, I . . . just don't do such things. Not in my book" (II, 131). The last four words suggest not moral scruples, but rather that relations with a woman are not to Bill's liking. Meanwhile he maintains his wit: "I'm going to be Minister for Home Affairs" (II, 131). Such distance is part of Bill's peculiar strength. He remains untouched by feelings, thus less susceptible to hurt.

James's idea of what he believes happened that night in Leeds must be fantasy, for Stella has not provided such information, at least within the time frame of the play. Thus the dwelling on sense detail may be wish fulfillment:

> You admired the room, it was so feminine, you felt awake, didn't feel like sleeping, you sat down, on the bed. She wanted you to go, you wouldn't. She

became upset, you sympathized, away from home, on a business trip, horrible life, especially for a woman, you comforted her, you have her solace, you stayed.   (II, 132)

From what little we have seen of James and Stella, we may assume that he is unable to give his wife the affection that he here imagines Bill has given her. Thus James attaches to Bill feelings that James cannot find within himself.

In defense Bill volunteers to "strip and show you my unscarred body" (II, 133). He senses James's reluctant interest. In return James refers to Bill as a "wag," then asks for a drink, and although at this point the homosexual attraction is explored no further, James's staying so long and reviewing Bill's patterns of behavior is a strong sign. Soon, however, James's frustration, whether at his inability either to arrive at the truth about his wife's behavior or to match Bill's social charm, takes the form of physical action, as James lunges forward and stands menacingly over Bill, who agrees to tell the "truth." First he admits to having met Stella; then he denies much of the story:

> The rest of it just didn't happen. I mean, I wouldn't do that sort of thing. I mean, that sort of thing . . . it's just meaningless. I can understand that you're upset, of course, but honestly, there was nothing else to it. Just a few kisses.   (II, 136)

Bill's confession may be taken as a momentary retreat or a mocking of James's desperation to clarify. In either case the impact of the scene on James is manifested when James later asks Stella for olives. The similarity to the earlier dialogue pattern with Bill intimates that James views both his wife and Bill from the same perspective, and that he is trying to dominate her the way he did Bill: "That must be the reason we've never had them in the house. You've simply never been interested enough in olives to ask whether I liked them or not" (II, 139). His anger is a sign of befuddlement, a result of uncertainty over his wife's actions in tandem with his own absorption with Bill. Of the four characters in this play, James is the one whose identity is most disjointed, as well as the one who is driven hardest to establish authority.

James is not alone in his doubt. Harry, too, is plagued by anxiety as he questions Bill about the visitor. Bill's answers mock Harry's anguish: "Oh . . . lemon hair, nigger brown teeth, wooden leg, bottlegreen eyes and a toupee. Know him?" (II, 140). Harry tries to assert his prerogatives: "Who is this man and what does he want?" (II, 140). But Harry's void and Bill's knowledge give Bill the power not to answer, a strength paralleled in the next scene as James interrogates Stella. He is struck especially by her lack of caring: "Do you mean anyone would have done? You mean it just happened to be him, but it might as well have been anyone?" (II, 141).

James's retaliation suggests his own ambiguous feelings and brings out Stella's as well. When James proposes going to see Bill, Stella tries to dissuade him: "Please don't go and see him" (II, 142). She wants to keep her extramarital relationship private. We cannot be certain if she actually values her friendship with Bill, or if she seeks to maintain an advantage over James by keeping him away from Bill. But James undercuts Stella by admitting to having met Bill. James also claims to have dined with him, as well as to have found Bill compatible: "We've got the same interests" (II, 142). James goes on to relate that Bill reminded him of an old school chum named Hawkins who, like Bill, was an opera fan, an enthusiasm James claims as his own: "Since James reveals that he is a secret opera fan, he may be admitting his own latent homosexuality, though because nothing develops along this line, he is probably just using the suggestion as a threat" (Gale, *Butter's Going Up*, 123). The first part of Gale's claim is accurate, but the second part ignores that the homosexuality may be a part of James that he wishes to suppress, and that this battle to achieve self-understanding is one more facet of his vulnerability. Moreover, James's constant references to manhood and masculinity may be intended to remind Stella that she is condemned to remain outside certain spheres of James's life. Or perhaps James is trying to bolster his male ego, now tottering in the face of Stella's secret or James's attraction to Bill.

James's return to visit Bill is an aggressive move, a desire perhaps to explore this aspect of himself that has thus far lain dormant, but which Bill has exposed. This desire is apparent especially when James invites Bill to stand with him before the mirror. James may be insinuating that he and Bill share something not immediately apparent, but that lies within them both. That quality may be a homosexual attraction. Part of James's weakness is that he cannot face these desires, while the source of Bill's power in his dealings with both James and Harry is that Bill knows precisely who he is. Thus he *"smiles, and turns up the radio"* (II, 146).

In the next scene this aspect of the relationship is paralleled to the tension between Harry and Stella. Harry has gone to confirm for himself the truth of Bill's meeting her, but even after Stella denies knowing Bill, Harry is compelled to talk about him:

> I found him in a slum, you know, by accident. Just happened to be in a slum one day, and there he was. I realized he had talent straight away. I gave him a roof, gave him a job, and he came up trumps. We've been close friends for years. (II, 147)

The speech is a combination of justification and desperation. Harry is explaining to Stella, but also to himself, the legitimacy of his feelings for Bill, as well as Bill's debt to him. He is also denigrating Bill so as to lessen Stella's possible interest, but the act reveals Harry's self-loathing, for even when he tries to dismiss Bill, Harry demonstrates his own shame at needing him. Stella's strength becomes clear when she denies even knowing Bill, while her description of a happy marriage undercuts James's story about him. Her success is also an example of power achieved through narrative.

The rest of the play reveals the plight of characters who do not know the truth, yet must battle to protect themselves from that gap in their knowledge. The struggle inevitably falls short, as is dramatized in the next scene. Bill taunts James about holding the cheese knife, a phallic symbol, and implies that James's reluctance to wield it suggests fear, perhaps of James's recognition of his desire for Bill: "Try it. Hold the blade. It won't cut you. Not if you handle it properly. Not if you grasp it firmly up to the hilt" (II, 150). Meanwhile Bill taunts James about Stella:

> You're a chap who's been married for two years, aren't you, happily? There's a bond of iron between you and your wife. It can't be corroded by a trivial thing like this. I've apologized, she's apologized. Honestly, what more can you want? (II, 151)

Then Bill mocks the marriage relationship in general:

> Every woman is bound to have an outburst of . . . wild sensuality at one time or another. That's the way I look at it, anyway. It's part of their nature. Even though it may be the kind of sensuality of which you yourself have never been the fortunate recipient. What? (*He laughs.*) That is a husband's fate, I suppose. Mind

you, I think it's the system that's at fault, not you. Perhaps she'll never need to
do it again, who knows?   (II, 151)

How intriguing that the possibly bisexual Bill is the one to explain the
dualities of a woman's nature.

The last two words of the speech above are the essence of James's agony.
Bill rests secure in knowledge: he is cognizant of what events transpired in
Leeds, and he is at ease with his own nature. James lacks awareness of both,
and in his inability to gain assurance, to gain power over himself or anyone
else, he is, like other Pinter men, reduced to the haplessness of violence. Thus
he tosses the knife at Bill, who blocks the blade, but cuts his hand.

This conflict is interrupted by Harry, who has been to the side listening.
Casually he embarks on a fabrication of his own, first diminishing the extent
of Bill's wound, then genially toasting: "Healthy minds in healthy bodies" (II,
153). As if by chance, he recounts his visit to Stella, then retreats behind the
comforting illusion Stella provided:

What she confessed was . . . that she'd made the whole thing up. She'd made
the whole damn thing up. For some odd reason of her own. They never met,
you see, Bill and your wife; they never even spoke. This is what Bill says, and
this is now what your wife admits. They had nothing whatever to do with
each other; they don't know each other. Women are very strange. But I
suppose you know more about that than I do; she's your wife. If I were you
I'd go home and knock her over the head with a saucepan and tell her not to
make up such stories again.   (II, 154)

The repetition of facts, the forced humor, and the attempt to foster masculine
camaraderie reflect Harry's insecurity. He knows that he is creating an
illusion, but he needs that illusion to survive the reality that humiliates him,
as he reveals in his description of Bill, an uglier, more violent, portrait than
he offered Stella:

There's something faintly putrid about him, don't you find? Like a slug.
There's nothing wrong with slugs in their place, but he's a slum slug; there's
nothing wrong with slum slugs in their place, but this one won't keep his
place—he crawls all over the walls of nice houses, leaving slime, don't you,

boy? He confirms stupid sordid stories just to amuse himself, while everyone else has to run around in circles to get to the root of the matter and smooth the whole thing out. (II, 155)

Clear from this speech is Harry's contempt for Bill, as well as his jealousy over him. Perhaps most important, the violence of Harry's imagery suggests his self-hatred, frustration with his own emotional and sexual void that can be filled only by young men like Bill.

Bill does not allow James and Harry to maintain even this illusion about events in question. Instead he upsets their comfort with yet one more narrative:

I never touched her . . . we sat . . . in the lounge, on a sofa . . . for two hours . . . talked . . . we talked about it . . . we didn't . . . move from the lounge . . . never went to her room . . . just talked . . . about what we would do . . . if we did get to her room . . . two hours . . . we never touched . . . we just talked about it . . . (II, 156–157)

The placement of this version and Bill's calm tone suggest that this story might be true. Certainly it seems logical in light of what we know about both Bill and Stella, for we may surmise that they had a great deal about which to talk. Each is a kept partner, each is often left alone, and each may need to converse openly and release desires normally under restraint. Furthermore, since Bill is homosexual, he may be more at ease with the feminine side of himself and offer Stella some of the sensibility, as well as the sympathy, that James denies her and that she craves. Finally, because of Bill's homosexuality, he and Stella may establish a relationship without the complication of sexual desire that in Pinter's works often creates a struggle for dominance between partners.

At this point, however, truth is no longer the issue—doubt is. Thus James leaves, and Harry is left to stare at Bill, who sits sucking his wounded hand with childlike innocence. But Bill's confession has more bite: "By saying that he talked with Stella about lovemaking, Bill is in fact telling Harry that he is dreaming of breaking away from him, of returning to a heterosexual life" (Esslin, *Pinter the Playwright*, 134). Therefore Bill's knowledge, linked with Harry's perpetual doubt about Bill's loyalties, leaves Bill with the power in their relationship. Similarly, James returns to his wife and asks a series of questions, hoping to ascertain the truth from her, but he receives no answer at all: "*STELLA looks at him, neither confirming nor denying*" (II, 157). She, too, recognizes the vulnerability caused by James's doubt. Pinter adds one more detail: "*Her face is friendly, sympathetic*" (II, 157). Perhaps Stella is willing to reconcile with James. At the same time she assumes a position of dominance based on knowledge:

> In the "*half light*" that ends the play, Pinter reveals the two couples, each reflective of the other, each containing a man shattered or insecure because his mate's response has made him uncertain of sexual fidelity, and therefore insecure about his relationship with his partner, who may become, because of his or her certainty, more dominant than before.   (Dukore, *Where Laughter Stops*, 33)

Bill and Stella most likely did not become partners out of a desire for dominance. To the contrary, their compatibility is apparent. Yet at the same time their own knowledge of themselves and their relationship, coupled with Harry's and James's uncertainty, creates power, although one diminished by economic need. Furthermore, James's uncertainty about his wife is compounded by confusion over his own fascination with Bill. Thus James's circle of doubt encompasses not only his wife, but himself.

The vulnerability borne by Harry and James is similar to the predicament of the Captain in Strindberg's *The Father*. When his wife, Laura, hints that the Captain can never verify the paternity of his daughter, doubt mushrooms inside his mind, and he turns this single issue into a questioning of all existence:

> Now there are only shadows, hiding in the bushes and sticking out their heads to laugh. It's like grappling with thin air, fighting with blank cartridges. A painful truth would have been a challenge, rousing body and soul to action, but now . . . my thoughts dissolve into mist, and my brain grinds emptiness until it catches fire!   (Strindberg, 47)

Within moments the Captain goes mad, broken by the combination of his wife's knowledge and his own eternal doubt.

Neither Harry nor James articulates the dilemma so acutely or floridly, but then Pinter's characters usually restrain themselves. Withholding emotion is one way to preserve a stronghold in the battleground that is the world of relationships. Nonetheless, the weakness of Harry and James is apparent in their questions, their pained wit, and their need to acquire knowledge, all a reflection of their insecurity. Bill understands himself and knows the truth about what has transpired, but he remains economically dependent and thus frustrated by his lack of control over his life. Although Stella has the strength of her female nature and knowledge of who she is and what has happened, her solitude reflects the dissolution of her life and the absence of love. All four characters struggle for power, and all four remain partially thwarted.

The Collection is a beautifully structured work, built on a matrix of oppositions between reality and illusion, love and jealousy, need and desire, comedy and pathos. Like the characters, the audience is perpetually out of balance. Our desire to know the truth is exacerbated by our realization that we never shall know it; our frustration is oddly soothed by that same realization.

3
—

The Lover

The ambivalence of our social selves, the coexistence in all of us of the primeval, amoral, instinct-dominated sensual being on one hand, and the tamed, regulated social conformist on the other, is one of the dominant themes of Pinter's writing . . .   (Esslin, *Pinter the Playwright*, 140)

This judgment relates particularly closely to *The Lover*, originally produced on television in 1963, then transferred to the stage later that year. The work dramatizes human beings possessed by warring instincts that underlie their struggle for identity. The play also suggests that certain of these instincts within men differ from those within women, and, moreover, that the social convention of marriage cannot control such qualities, which manifest themselves in struggles for power.

The beginning of the play is innocuous, as Sarah is in the midst of household cleaning. She wears a *"crisp, demure dress"* (*The Lover*, II, 161) that implies that she is performing the traditional wifely role. When Richard enters, he kisses her *"on the cheek"* (II, 161), another gesture that denotes conventional domestic bliss. With the opening words, however, that image is shattered, as Richard asks *"amiably"*: "Is your lover coming today?" (II, 161). Immediately one tension of the play is established: that between uncivilized passion and constricting societal decorum. From this point on Sarah and Richard both undergo an internal struggle, initially disguising desires under polite chatter, then using a series of ritualized games to stimulate their marriage. At the same time they release yearnings that under normal social conditions remain checked. A corollary tension is that even as the two seem to achieve marital equilibrium, other forces inside them take over.

Richard's opening question that evening seems to have little effect, as for a few moments he and Sarah banter agreeably. She asks, "Bad traffic?" and he responds genially, "No. Quite good traffic, actually" (II, 162). The dialogue remains light until Richard injects the first note of strain: "Did you show him the hollyhocks?" (II, 163). Sarah's pause and her repetition of the word "hollyhocks" indicate that she may be taken aback, and Richard's continual questions keep her on the defensive. This pattern dominates the play. Sarah seems content with the complex relationship she and Richard have established, but Richard invariably becomes dissatisfied, and his cease-less aggression reflects his battle to retain power. This rationale explains a portion of Richard's action. A more complicated question that pervades the play is why he reacts as aggressively as he does.

Richard proceeds to ask Sarah about her behavior with her lover: "You didn't move to another room?" (II, 164). Despite his convivial manner, Richard slowly reveals himself to be jealous of this other man in her life: "Does it ever occur to you that while you're spending the afternoon being unfaithful to me I'm sitting at a desk going through balance sheets and graphs?" (II, 165). He seems resentful of Sarah's assignation, and we suspect that his veneer of sophistication masks profound anxiety.

Sarah's first reply appears cold: "It makes it all the more piquant" (II, 165). We cannot tell whether she is playing or attempting to assert herself. Her second reply a few moments later raises a new issue: "But it's you I love" (II, 166). After his query she repeats the line, apparently trying to comfort him, but the ramifications are intriguing, for she is implying that the schism in her life between husband and lover also represents the distinction between love and sex.

Is this separation a source of power? If so, then Sarah resembles Ruth in *The Homecoming*, for whom sex is no more than a business, and who manages simultaneously to conceal or control all emotion. Sarah, however, is different from Ruth. Sarah makes clear that she feels deep affection for Richard, but that she has emotional or physical needs he cannot satisfy. Does the need arise out of some deficiency of Richard's? The answer turns out to be no. The need, in fact, is revealed to be inherent in the nature of marriage as Pinter dramatizes it. The play also suggests that something within Sarah demands that she go outside the legally sanctioned bounds of matrimony for fulfillment of certain longings. Furthermore, Richard has his own unique needs, and as such he acts according to a vision of women common to many of Pinter's male characters: that females play a double role, split between wife and whore, between respectable and illicit, between maternal and sexual. Richard seems to relish this duality, for it intensifies the passions of his marriage; yet at the same time it frustrates him, for it gives Sarah a psychological edge that leads to power within their relationship. Thus the inevitable tension that rises from this role-playing.

When Richard turns his attention to Sarah's shoes, one sign of her role of the moment, she apologizes and changes them, apparently to diffuse his resentment of her lover's presence. Yet Sarah intensifies Richard's pain by mentioning a new piece of evidence: "I knew you were with your mistress" (II, 167). Ostensibly she seeks to comfort Richard by reminding him that he has an extramarital relationship of his own, one she tolerates with equanimity. Richard, however, does not accept this solicitude. Instead he responds with renewed aggression: "But I haven't got a mistress. I'm very well acquainted with a whore, but I haven't got a mistress. There's a world of difference" (II, 167). Sarah tries to maintain composure by suggesting that this other woman must have redeemable qualities, but Richard continues to talk of her in crude terms, clarifying her appeal: "You can't sensibly inquire whether a whore is witty. It's of no significance whether she is or she isn't. She's simply a whore, a functionary who either pleases or displeases" (II, 168). Richard is attempting to exert strength by showing how dispassionately he feels about the woman he sees. His depersonalization of her should be understood as an attempt to prove his superiority to Sarah, who has shown that she can separate sex with her lover from the emotional bond with Richard. Now Richard fights back, implying that he is even more emotionally detached than Sarah:

I wasn't looking for your double, was I? I wasn't looking for a woman I could respect, as you, whom I could admire and love, as I do you. Was I? All I wanted

was . . . how shall I put it . . . someone who could express and engender lust with
all lust's cunning. Nothing more.   (II, 169)

This crucial speech reveals both Richard's need for dominance and his inevitable failure to achieve it. On the one hand, he reaffirms his capacity to indulge
in sex without love. To do so is, in the context of this dramatic situation, a
source of strength. At the same time his need to question, in conjunction with
his need to explain, reveals that he requires Sarah's approval. He is trying to
hurt her; yet his effort to be casual, undercut by his inability to be casual, shows
weakness. And his extensive explanation, including "express and engender," is
further self-justification, another sign of weakness.

This dichotomy in Richard, this combination of strength and need, takes
the form of a relentless inquisition of Sarah about her lover. Her method of
comfort is peculiar: "But I must say he's very loving. His whole body emanates
love" (II, 172). At this point the line seems harsh, a confession that her lover
provides an emotional release that Richard cannot offer. Ironically, though,
the sentiment, in unity with other generous remarks about the lover, calms
Richard, who denies jealousy (II, 173). Finally Sarah ends the scene with a
statement of reassurance: "Because I think things are beautifully balanced,
Richard" (II, 173).

The interlude with the milkman suggests the blandness of Sarah's existence outside her life with Richard. She is dressed provocatively, anticipating
Richard's arrival, when she notices that she is wearing low-heeled shoes, and
so she rushes to change. Yet when the bell rings, the milkman appears. Even
in this brief interlude Pinter injects tension, for while Sarah is frustrated that
the delivery is late and may interrupt her meeting with Richard, the milkman
almost challenges her refusal to accept cream. In this brief tableau, which
represents life outside her marriage, Sarah must be demure and accept the
milkman's attitude, which borders on insolence. Only with Richard can Sarah
release her more passionate, more powerful, aspect. Thus we are again
reminded that her marital arrangement satisfies her.

The moment when the profound irony of the play becomes clear is when
Richard enters to Sarah's greeting: "Hallo, Max" (II, 175). Now we realize
that Sarah and Richard indulge in an elaborate fantasy, and now we understand why Richard was soothed at Sarah's compliments about the warmth of
her lover. We also understand the relaxed tone of much of the earlier

proceedings. But questions remain, and the most important revolves around Richard: if he is the lover of whom Sarah has spoken, why is he jealous?

The answer remains unclarified for some time. First the two participate in a nonverbal ritual, as they tap the bongo and embrace sensually in a scene reminiscent of Stanley's beating of the drum in *The Birthday Party*. In both plays the action and sounds imply a primitive force unable to surface amid constraints of civilization. Here it also reflects the passionate side of the human spirit and contributes to the play's portrait of the contrast between a marriage devoid of sex and an extramarital relationship fired by passionate sex.

What follows is a series of fantasy scenes, a theme-and- variations of sexual infidelity. In the text Pinter identifies Richard as Max, as if to ensure that the audience and perhaps the actors regard this figure as a different personage. At first Max seems to trap Sarah and threaten rape, while she protests that she is waiting for her husband. That this episode is the first game played may be Pinter's implication that what Sarah finds most alluring is the illicit quality of the fantasy. Max then turns into a savior, and the familiar image of a woman in danger rescued by a gallant swain takes over. Soon Sarah becomes more aggressive, and when Max protests that he has a wife, Sarah becomes downright abusive, exacerbating the level of competition. Here is a moment where she holds authority. A moment later Max claims to trap Sarah, who protests that she is helpless to respond: "I'm a married woman. You can't treat me like this" (II, 179). Max also refers to Sarah as "Dolores" (II, 178), then "Mary" (II, 179), name changes that temporarily give Sarah the freedom of identity Max enjoys. At that point his pursuit becomes relentless. Thus within a few minutes the two run the gamut of roles within a sadomasochistic relationship, playing dominant and submissive to each other.

The relationship may be judged bizarre, but nonetheless it seems mutually satisfying. That impression is destroyed, however, when Max, apparently as part of the game, asks about Sarah's husband. She comments that Richard has known "for years" (II, 180) about her relationship with Max and doesn't mind, but Max blurts out, "Well, I'm beginning to mind" (II, 180), then "It's got to stop. It can't go on" (II, 181). When Sarah responds, "Are you serious?" (II, 181), we cannot be sure whether she asks the question as Max's lover or as Richard's wife.

At first Max blames his dissatisfaction on his own wife:

She thinks I know a whore, that's all. Some spare-time whore, that's all.   (II, 181)

She'd mind if she knew that, in fact . . . I've got a full-time mistress, two or three
times a week, a woman of grace, elegance, wit, imagination—   (II, 182)

The tension is within Max himself. Or within Richard. Sarah tries to comfort
Max: "She doesn't mind, she wouldn't mind—she's happy, she's happy" (II,
182). Here Sarah speaks as and for herself. Yet Max still threatens to take his
case to Richard: "We're both men. You're just a bloody woman" (183).
Richard thereby belittles Sarah's feelings, trying to turn her into an object
for his pleasure in whatever role he chooses. He also bewilders her, maintaining his place in the battle for power within the relationship.

Thus when Sarah angrily demands to know whether he is playing a game,
Max is blunt: "I've played my last game" (II, 183). His way of ending the day's
performance is to express dissatisfaction with Sarah: "You're too bony" (II, 184).
Then: "You're not plump enough. You're nowhere near plump enough. You
know what I like. I like enormous women" (II, 184). Sarah cannot believe that
he is destroying the illusionary world they have created: "You're having a lovely
joke" (II, 185). Max's destruction, however, is purposeful: "It's no joke" (II, 185).

The key to Max's disenchantment is revealed in the final scene, when
Richard returns that night, remorseful. After Sarah expresses disappointment
with Max, Richard mocks his own behavior: "I mean if I, for instance, were
called upon to fulfill the function of a lover and felt disposed, shall we say,
to accept the job, well, I'd as soon give it up as be found incapable of executing
its proper and consistent obligation" (II, 186). He extols Sarah: "Yes, I find
you very beautiful. I have great pride in being seen with you. When we're
out to dinner, or at the theater" (II, 187). He even contradicts Max's judgment
about Sarah's appearance: "I'm fond of thin ladies" (II, 188).

Is Richard jealous of himself as lover, as Burkman suggests (Burkman, *The
Dramatic World of Harold Pinter,* 106)? Possibly. But Elin Diamond focuses on
Sarah's next line, "I thought the contrary" (II, 188), and concludes that
because Sarah now recalls the earlier game, she is playing into Richard's hands
(Diamond, *Pinter's Comic Play,* 129). This analysis appears to come closer to
the core of the play: the competition for power. In the ongoing game Richard

plays two distinct roles: himself and Max. Sarah, however, almost always plays herself. As a woman she has two entirely different, yet complementary, aspects to her own personality: wife and lover. Richard, though, must become another person to participate in this charade. Perhaps he envies his wife's capacity to find in herself what Richard can only find in a different mask; thus his inevitable frustration with the performance.

After all, in the role of Max, Richard plays Sarah's game. Her name changes for only a brief time, and several of her fantasies are fulfilled, while Richard serves primarily to satisfy the multiplicity of her needs. Now, in "reality," so to speak, he is in charge, determining the course of action. Thus he tries to end the other game by decreeing that Sarah's "debauchery" must stop (II, 189).

Sarah attempts to sustain the illicit relationship: "I didn't take my lover ten years ago. Not quite. Not on the honeymoon" (II, 190). She insinuates that her love for Richard himself is and always has been paramount, that she has played the game only to satisfy Richard, and she praises his willingness to conform to her desires: "You've always understood" (II, 190). Richard, though, is adamant: "If I find him on these premises I'll kick his teeth out" (II, 191). He claims to have paid off his own whore because she was too bony (II, 191–192). Thus he is dispensing with all illusions, the variety of sexual adventures that Sarah has found so arousing. This way he will be the figure of authority, and that power gives him security and identity.

His final gesture of destruction is to take out the drum. In doing so he forces the worlds of fantasy and reality to clash, and the result devastates Sarah, who speaks *"with quiet anguish"*: "You've no right to question me. No right at all. It was our arrangement. No questions of this kind. Please. Don't don't. It was our arrangement" (II, 193). Her reaction reflects psychologist Judith Bardwick's portrait of certain aspects of female emotional and sexual desire:

> She will need to be reassured that she is precious and loved and that by loving she is being good. Her lack of self-esteem will make affiliation very important and sex an emotionally loaded useful tool for garnering love. But this will also be a source of danger because if she uses sex in order to create love she may feel she is prostituting and degrading herself. (Bardwick, 69)

This description fits Sarah's behavior, for while she participates in this series of games in order to share Richard's life and receive his love, at moments such as this the entire enterprise frustrates her. Thus when Richard does not relent, Sarah has no recourse but to assert her own power:

> I have other visitors, other visitors, all the time, I receive all the time. Other afternoons, all the time. When neither of you know, neither of you. I give them strawberries in season. With cream. Strangers, total strangers. But not to me, not while they're here. They come to see the hollyhocks. And then they stay for tea. Always. Always.   (II, 193)

The reference to cream recalls the scene with the delivery man, and the mention of hollyhocks refers to Richard's early question that initiated the struggle for command. Sarah seizes irrelevant bits and facts, then through narrative creation turns them into irrefutable fantasy, her own vehicle for achieving power.

When she becomes the aggressor, Richard goes along with her story, scratching the drum to signify his willingness to participate. Then he approaches her: "You can't get out, darling. You're trapped" (II, 195). Again he is the sexual predator. Far from being dismayed, however, she giggles and reverts to her role: "You're very forward. You really are. Oh, you really are. But my husband will understand. My husband does understand" (II, 195). We cannot be certain if she is talking to Richard, Max, or a new, unnamed creation: "You usually wear something else, don't you? Take off your jacket" (II, 195-196). This line, though, sparks a challenge within Richard, as she brings a new dimension to the competition. When she volunteers to change her own clothes, Richard is taken with her boldness and agrees to take part in this new charade, concluding the play by referring to her as "You lovely whore" (II, 196). Once again the game resumes.

Several critics have noted the similarity between this play and the works of Jean Genet, which are also built upon levels of fantasy. George Wellwarth, however, suggests a key difference: "To Genet human beings are composed of layer upon layer of illusion draped upon a nonexistent core; to Pinter human beings are simply inscrutable, to themselves as well as to others" (Wellwarth, 236). Another important difference is that Genet's characters are consciously striving to play out illusions of power. They are aware that for them the struggle to create a satisfying fantasy life is more fulfilling than whatever passes for reality. In *The Maids*, for instance, Solange broods over the failure to make the ritual work: "The same thing happens every time. And it's all your fault, you're never ready. I can't finish you off" (Genet, 46). In *The Lover*, however, the need for fantasy is unspoken. The rules are never articulated. The game is an extension of life, not a substitute for it.

The alternation between fantasy and reality that dominates *The Lover* also brings to mind the illusionary life carried on in Edward Albee's *Who's Afraid of Virginia Woolf.* For the rest of the world George and Martha act as though they have a child; only in private do they acknowledge the truth. Sarah and Richard, however, maintain their roles even in privacy. They are not acting for others. They lives are performance. Furthermore, in Albee's play, the fantasy world is ultimately thrown aside, and at the end George and Martha join in love, prepared to face reality together. In *The Lover* the world of fantasy is maintained, and the matter of supremacy or union is less clear. Indeed, the ambiguous nature of the ending has caused considerable disparity of critical interpretation.

Sakellaridou tries to place the play in the framework of her overall feminist vision: "[Pinter] lets [Sarah] assert her ego in the limited space of personal relations within which she is confined, thus proving the strength of her personality and the vitality of her imagination" (Sakellaridou, 105). This claim, however, fails to take into account that Richard's capacity for fantasy is at least as powerful as Sarah's. Other critics disagree sharply about the winner. Diamond asserts that "Richard wins. Not because he destroys the game, but because he plays for 'real'" (Diamond, *Pinter's Comic Play*, 130). Dukore, on the other hand, suggests that "although [Sarah] says, in the seduction game she persuades him to play, that she is trapped by him, it is Richard who is trapped by her. His role of lover invades and dominates his marital world" (Dukore, *Harold Pinter*, 69). This vision of Richard as victim is supported by Burkman: "But as the play concentrates on Richard's desire to integrate the roles played by himself and his wife, Sarah's need to continue their compartmentalized existence is fully examined. Her need, in fact, proves stronger and dominates as the play ends" (Burkman, *The Dramatic World of Harold Pinter*, 105). Another perspective is offered by Gale, who comments that Sarah and Richard are mutual victims: "The paradox is that the two people involved must play the game if they are to harmonize areas in their own natures, forcing reality to fit their theories, but in doing so they subordinate themselves to the identity of the game" (Gale, *Butter's Going Up*, 136).

Gale's analysis seems most acute but does not take into consideration that the game itself is dramatized as the product of biological compulsion. For both Sarah and Richard, the games are a unifying force that provides structure for their lives and from which they take an odd comfort. The characters also find in their performances individual satisfaction. Sarah regards marriage as a legal sanction, a method of ordering her own life, and a reflection of the Apollonian element in her character. The world of fantasy is the Dionysian side, the release of drives and desires that ordinarily she would have to sublimate. Richard uses marriage to give himself an attractive partner whom he may hold up before others as a sign of his respectability and worldly success. The games he plays bring to his life a male version of what Sarah enjoys: stimulating variety, as he enjoys encounters with a wife, a mistress, and a prostitute.

However, Pinter also dramatizes that Richard is seized by an additional need, one that these particular games do not satisfy. He needs to be in command of the marriage, to have power over his wife. When Sarah is pleased that all is in balance, she implies that she and Richard are equals, but at that point he becomes dissatisfied and rejects the game so as to rob her of her release and to subjugate her to the conventions of marriage. When at the end of the play she challenges back, creating memories that threaten his position, he is forced to resume the competition. The reversion to role-playing is thus the inevitable product of biological drives within the two characters, as James Hollis notes: "The conclusion presents two people who have finally awakened to their deepest desires. They have found, among other things, an atavistic violence as part of their sexuality, a violence in which one is master and the other mastered" (Hollis, 68). The two are locked in a perpetual struggle for dominance within the social structure of marriage, and the game itself is a mechanism for equilibrium. As long as the two struggle, as long as no resolution is achieved, both can fulfill desires and retreat into the security of identity that they fabricate. Thus resolution is not only impossible, but also undesirable, for if either is in charge, then the other is dissatisfied. Even if equality is achieved temporarily, Richard is frustrated and must exert his own will. Consequently the game and the struggle are permanent.

Finally, The Lover questions the theatricality of all human relationships, and specifically those between men and women. To what extent do we always act, continually shifting from one mask to another? As we move each day through a series of confrontations with different individuals, we play a corresponding series of parts: child, parent, sibling, partner, lover, rival. Similarly, within a single relationship, our moods and attitudes change almost as frequently as the circumstances under which we function. Consequently, do we, consciously or unconsciously, take on several roles, switching from one to the other to fulfill different needs and longings? Is the sum of our identity, ultimately, this series of masks? While these questions do not pervade Pinter's work, they are raised provocatively in *The Lover*.

4

The Homecoming

Since its premiere in 1965, *The Homecoming* has remained the most controversial of Pinter's plays. In 1967 Walter Kerr wrote that the dramatist "has dragged us all, aching, through a half-drugged dream" (Kerr, *New York Times*, 6 January 1967), while Simon Trussler has claimed that *The Homecoming* is the only work of Pinter's "by which I have felt myself actually soiled and diminished" (Trussler, 134). Yet despite all the disparagement, the play remains fascinating, particularly regarding the relationship between power and identity, as characters struggle to gain authority within the family structure. One front of the war is fought among the men, but the key conflict is between these men and the lone woman who invades their home.

What Ruby Cohn refers to as "the jungle atmosphere of this home" (Cohn, 80) begins at once with the territorial demand from Max that Lenny surrender the newspaper: "Like two animals testing each other, one pokes and prods until the other swipes; neither draws blood" (Diamond, *Pinter's Comic Play*, 141). The antagonism between father and son is apparent from virtually the first words, and the familiar Pinter technique of unanswered, then repeated, questions separated by pauses reveals quickly that Max is the weaker figure. He asks for a cigarette, only to be ignored, but then he takes one from his pocket. Perhaps Max's question is a cry for attention or the act of a father seeking to ensure that his son continues to follow orders. Lenny, however, refuses to be submissive; instead, he has sufficient strength to establish his security with brief, sharp replies. Max bullies and threatens, but his stick is a cruel parody of age and fading masculine strength. As he himself admits: "I'm getting old, my word of honour" (*The Homecoming*, III, 24). Thus the family is in disorder. In Gerald Mast's witty image: "No wonder the old barnyard is restless; the cock-of-the-walk is doddering" (Mast, 268).

The reference to MacGregor leads Max to recall his public and business life: "We were two of the worst hated men in the West End of London. I tell you, I still got the scars" (III, 24). We also note the reference to MacGregor's interest in Jessie, Lenny's mother. More disturbing, though, are Max's memories of his wife: "Mind you, she wasn't such a bad woman. Even though it made me sick just to look at her rotten stinking face, she wasn't such a bad bitch. I gave her the best bleeding years of my life" (III, 25). The combination of roughhouse affection and vulgar contempt reflects part of the complex male attitude toward women in this play.

The diatribe arouses further anger from Lenny, and he and Max go at each other briefly, but almost at once the conversation softens as the two reflect about horses. Despite their antagonism, the men share a bond. We soon learn that it is at one level professional, but more profoundly, it is one between father and son. No matter how bitterly rivalry separates the two, Max and Lenny understand each other. Their place as males in the same family, as well as their relationship with Jessie, means that they are inextricably tied in ways more profound than is possible between individuals from two different families, including husband and wife. Indeed, one of the key images of the text is that of "blood." The word suggests not only the liquid that flows through the body, as well as the remnants of activity in their butcher shop, but the "blood" ties shared by the family. No matter how great the enmity between these men, they share social and ethical values as well as a biological heritage.

Max's extended speech about horses starts innocently, but as he becomes more graphic we feel subtler implications:

But I was always able to tell a good filly by one particular trick. I'd look her in the eye. You see? I'd stand in front of her and look her straight in the eye, it was a kind of hypnotism, and by the look deep down in her eye I could tell whether she was a stayer or not. It was a gift. I had a gift.   (III, 26)

The word "trick" has implications of prostitution, and that usage reveals Max's attitude toward women. The crucial standard by which he judges them is how effectively they fulfill that role. His claims of expertise, though, arouse Lenny's ire. He questions Max's cooking, satirizing his father's role as the woman of the home, and when Max mutters about physical retaliation, Lenny mocks the feebleness of the threat:

> Oh, Daddy, you're not going to use your stick on me, are you? Eh? Don't use your stick on me Daddy. No, please. It wasn't my fault, it was one of the others. I haven't done anything wrong, Dad, honest. Don't clout me with that stick, Dad. (III, 27)

Lenny mimics what must have been the cries of fear he uttered when he was younger and suffered Max's punishment with that stick. Now Lenny is dominant, and like a younger primate standing over a defeated older male, he revels in power. Max's only response is silence.

Here Sam enters, the driver for the firm, but as a childless bachelor, outside the squabble for biological dominance. In social units throughout the animal kingdom, a male who does not father offspring forfeits his most fundamental masculine prerogative, and such creatures are outcasts. So, too, is Sam mocked by the others for his noncombatant status. Yet his alienation gives him knowledge that he uses as his form of power. For instance, when he claims to be aware of other men who have taken liberties in his car, Max immediately wants names, but Sam remains noncommittal (III, 31). We, however, think about Jessie and Mac. Furthermore, Sam's digression about his having "escorted" Jessie (III, 32) suggests that he knows secrets, that as Max's brother he is still inextricably tied to the family. As he says, "It was my pleasure" (III, 32).

The entrance of Joey, who immediately asks for food, brings another animalistic element. Even Max recognizes the parallel: "They walk in here every time of the day and night like bloody animals. Go and find yourself a mother" (III, 32). Indeed, references to beasts dominate the language of the play. One consequence of this aspect is an ever-present irony built on the contrast between images of animals and expressions of familial affection. Here, for example, Lenny taunts his father's feminized role: "What the boys want, Dad, is your own special brand of cooking, Dad. That's what the boys look forward to. The special understanding of food, you know, that you've got" (III, 33). Max resists the label "Dad," as if ashamed of his role as parent, but his anger also intimates that he is uncertain that he is in fact their true father. This suspicion gains credence at Sam's comment about his escorting Jessie: "You wouldn't have trusted any of your other brothers. You wouldn't have trusted Mac, would you? But you trusted me. I want to remind you" (III, 34). Sam adds: "He was a lousy stinking rotten loudmouth. A bastard uncouth sodding runt. Mind you, he was a good friend of yours" (III, 34). Perhaps Sam's implication is that Max and Mac shared more than the similarity of their names, specifically, the affections of Jessie. The scene also clarifies Max's resentment of Joey:

> I'll tell you what you've got to do. What you've got to do is you've got to learn how to defend yourself, and you've got to learn how to attack. That's your only trouble as a boxer. You don't know how to defend yourself, and you don't know how to attack.   (III, 33)

The derogation of Joey's skills hint at the frustrations of an old man who has lost his youthful vigor and is reduced to mocking the efforts of others. His insults have still another purpose:

> Max continually reminds his sons that they are still dependent on him. Somewhat like Pinter's smothering mother-figures, he wants to keep his sons as children. If they are dependent on him, he will maintain his dominant position. And in some ways he has kept them as children. As much as they hate Max, they do not leave their childhood home, although they are grown men.   (Osherow, 426)

Max's contempt for Sam serves a similar end: to keep Sam in a subordinate position. Sam points out that the house they live in belonged to their mother and therefore now belongs to both of them. Max, however, is concerned more with memories of his father:

> He'd bend right over me, then he'd pick me up. I was only that big. Then he'd dandle me. Give me the bottle. Wipe me clean. Give me a smile. Pat me on the bum. Pass me around, pass me from hand to hand. Toss me up in the air. Catch me coming down. I remember my father.   (III, 35)

The speech begins as a tribute, but as details accumulate Max is pained by memories of helplessness, of affection turning into abuse. Max hated his father's taunting, and we sense that when the opportunity arose to gain authority over him, Max took it. Now Max is in a similar position of vulnerability against his own son Lenny, who is gradually usurping Max's place at home, in business, and in life.

Thus the conflict between generations of males continues. Sam and Max, older and physically weaker, still possess certain prerogatives of age. Lenny and Joey are challenging their elders, but Joey lacks the intellect to use his strength and therefore functions only as an extension of Lenny's mind. At this point the battle has taken on a kind of inevitability, as the irresistible decline of one generation is accompanied by the equally irresistible rise of another. This cycle is interrupted with the entrance of one female; now instead of fighting strictly over territory, the males begin to fight additionally for possession of her.

What strikes us first about Ruth is her equanimity. She seems at ease entering a strange house, while Teddy, who ostensibly should be relaxed as he comes home, is tense. He talks incessantly, posing questions and seeking reassurance, while Ruth speaks and acts with confidence. When Teddy asks if Ruth is cold, she answers simply "No" (III, 37). Nor does she want anything to drink. Teddy, meanwhile, babbles:

> What do you think of the room? Big, isn't it? It's a big house. I mean, it's a fine room, don't you think? Actually there was a wall, across there . . . with a door. We knocked it down . . . years ago . . . to make an open living area. The structure wasn't affected, you see. My mother was dead. (III, 37)

The first sentences imply that Teddy is trying to comfort Ruth, but the underlying tone hints that he is whistling in the dark, trying just as hard to bolster himself. The last sentence, however, raises a few possibilities. Perhaps he means that his mother was the foundation of the household, or perhaps that without her the structure of the house was no longer the same. In any case, Teddy's insecurity is apparent in every line, as his rhythms and tone of speech contradict the apparent meaning of his words. Most important, the episode reinforces, sometimes comically, that the power in this relationship belongs to Ruth. For instance Teddy rambles: "Look, it's all right, really. I'm here. I mean . . . I'm with you. There's no need to be nervous. Are you nervous?" (III, 39). To which Ruth replies once more: "No" (III, 39). In retrospect we may look at Teddy's words "I'm with you" as more of an attempt to claim possession than as an offer of solace.

This suspicion is reinforced when Teddy asks Ruth for the third time about whether she is tired. At first Ruth says she is (III, 36). The second time she modifies her feelings: "Just a little" (III, 37). The third time she states simply "No" (III, 38), and presently announces her intention to take a walk. Apparently this house revitalizes her, and Teddy cannot stop her: "But what am I going to do?" (III, 40). The pause following this line emphasizes that in spite of the intellectual wall Teddy has built around himself, he is isolated and in need of the emotional buttressing Ruth has provided. Instead Ruth reassures him: "I won't go far. I'll come back" (III, 40). She is beyond Teddy's control, and he can only plead that she will remain with him, both at this particular moment and metaphorically in the marriage. At this point we might wonder why Ruth needs to walk the streets. In retrospect, the action is that of a professional staking out territory. Thus Teddy's fears later become more understandable.

In an intriguing article about the names that various Pinter characters share, Bernard Dukore reflects on the similarities between Teddy and Edward in *A Slight Ache*. Both operate with detachment, yet with latent hostility. After a substantial comparison and contrast of the two characters, Dukore concludes: "Although suppositions are not certainties, the intellectual Teddy seems to be another side of the intellectual Edward: more controlled, more cunning, more successful" (Dukore, "What's in a Name," 177). Dukore also correctly points out the most direct and important implications of Ruth's name: "In a partly ironic manner, it suggests the word 'ruth' (pity), and it also evokes the Biblical Ruth, whose husband's people become her people" (Dukore, "What's in a Name," 174).

The brief meeting between Teddy and Lenny is openly hostile. Teddy explains: "I've . . . just come back for a few days" (III, 42), to which Lenny replies offhandedly: "Oh yes? Have you?" (III, 42). Perhaps the two grew up as brothers, but given the differences in personality we might speculate that they have different fathers.

The early-morning encounter between Ruth and Lenny is a remarkable scene, as the two compete verbally for power. Lenny's need to talk, like

Teddy's earlier, suggests weakness, while Ruth's strength again is manifested in her placidity. When Lenny brings Ruth a glass of water from which she takes a sip, the action may be seen as a gesture of intimacy. Yet Ruth's refusal to thank Lenny or to place herself in any way in his debt blunts the proposal. We also note Lenny's unwillingness to deal with Ruth's marriage to Teddy. Twice she mentions it, and each time Lenny ignores her, suggesting that to his way of thinking, or at least the way of thinking he wants to present to Ruth, the relationship is meaningless. One more unnerving element is, as Lenny notes, that he wears pajamas, while Ruth is fully clothed. Lenny pretends the situation is humorous, for in his job he is accustomed to seeing women wearing nightclothes. Nonetheless, in this reversal he takes on the demeanor of a little boy before his mother.

Lenny's comments on imagining himself a soldier in Venice may be taken as masculine bravado, for they are followed by a bold request to hold Ruth's hand. When she questions "Why?" (III, 46), she insinuates that he does not have the capacity to proceed further. This slur on his manhood inspires from Lenny an extended monologue: "One night, not too long ago, one night down by the docks, I was standing alone under an arch, watching all the men jibbing the boom, out in the harbor, and playing about the yardarm . . ." (III, 46). The opening words suggest a fairy tale or some other equally fanciful narrative, while the phony cant about actions of the sailors implies more strongly that the story is at least part fantasy. It may be a composite of several events. Whatever its origin, it demonstrates Lenny's knowledge of the London underworld, as well as his potential violence toward women. Lenny claims that the woman made a proposal to him and that "normally I would have subscribed to it. I mean I would have subscribed to it in the normal course of events. The only trouble was she was falling apart with the pox" (III, 46). He contemplated killing her, he announces, without fear of the chauffeur (we assume he means Sam), but then decided merely to brutalize her.

Lenny no doubt intends the story to communicate power over women, his right to assault a female of whom he disapproves. When Ruth asks how he knew the woman was diseased, Lenny sneers: "I decided she was" (III, 47). This admission also seems intended to be a statement of authority. The boast is more likely, however, a confession that either the entire incident has been concocted, or that Lenny has related his own version of such a meeting.

Furthermore, that Lenny chooses to demonstrate his manhood with a narrative in which he does not conquer a woman sexually, but instead beats and kicks her, implies that he is impotent.

The second anecdote also reflects Lenny's latent brutality, this time against an old woman:

> So after a few minutes I said to her, now look here, why don't you stuff this iron mangle up your arse? Anyway, I said, they're out of date, you want a spin drier. I had a good mind to give her a workover there and then, but as I was feeling jubilant with the snow-clearing I just gave her a short-arm jab to the belly and jumped on a bus outside. (III, 49)

The first story depicts violence against a younger woman, a prostitute. This second relates violence taken against an older woman, a maternal figure. Through narrative, therefore, Lenny attacks both aspects of Ruth's personality, and also he demonstrates savagery. Yet he fails to prove his sexual capacity, especially as he recalls running away after striking the old woman.

Ruth intuits this weakness. She refuses his request for the glass, then refers to him as "Leonard" (III, 49), the name, as Lenny warns, his mother gave him. Sensing fear, Ruth becomes more aggressive: "If you take the glass . . . I'll take you" (III, 50). Lenny retreats almost at once, sputtering the way Teddy did earlier: "You're in love anyway, with another man. You've had a secret liaison with another man. His family didn't even know. Then you come here without a word of warning and start to make trouble" (III, 50). When he indulged in monologues, Lenny's sentence structure was elaborate, the style of a man of assurance. Now, under threat, Lenny resorts to the choppy prose of retreat, chattering rather than expostulating. Ruth's femaleness, her identity as woman, wife, mother, and, most likely, whore, leaves Lenny helpless. As her advances become more blatant, his blusters make his fears both more desperate and more comic.

The profound impression Ruth makes is evident in the question Lenny later asks Max:

> That night . . . you know . . . the night you got me . . . that night with Mum, what was it like? Eh? When I was just a glint in your eye. What was it like? What was the background to it? I mean, I want to know the real facts about

my background. I mean, for instance, is it a fact that you had me in mind all
the time, or is it a fact that I was the last thing you had in mind? (III, 52)

Ruth's presence and attitude have spurred Lenny to think about Jessie. His
question suggests his sexual desire for both women, but his earlier behavior
with Ruth communicated apprehension. These conflicting instincts recur in
all the men in this play. They are attracted to women, yet fearful of them;
contemptuous, yet submissive. They remain brutal to one another, as in Max's
blunt response to Lenny: "You'll drown in your own blood" (III, 52). On one
level the line is sheer insult. On another level it hints that Lenny's family
history will destroy him.

Before Ruth appears the next morning, Max berates Sam's lack of virility:

> We took you into the butcher's shop, you couldn't even sweep the dust off the
> floor. We took MacGregor into the shop, he could run the place by the end of
> a week. Well, I'll tell you one thing. I respected my father not only as a man but
> as a number one butcher! And to prove it I followed him into the shop. I learned
> to carve a carcass at his knee. I commemorated his name in blood. I gave birth
> to three grown men! All on my own bat. What have you done? (III, 55–56)

The speech has curious overtones. One, a butcher shop is a meat market and
may be a euphemism for the family's prostitution business. Two, the place of
MacGregor in that business implies that he became part of the family, again
suggesting he had relations with Jessie. Three, the reference to blood,
undercut by Max's peculiar insistence on his giving birth to three sons, hints
at uncertainty about their paternity.

The appearance of Ruth sets Max off: "We've had a smelly scrubber in my
house all night. We've had a stinking pox-ridden slut in my house all night"
(III, 57). His professional eye is struck immediately, but his reaction grows
more complicated: "I've never had a whore under this roof before. Ever since
your mother died" (III, 58). His tribute to the memory of his wife has a double
implication: perhaps he has never brought a whore into the house, or perhaps
Jessie was the last he allowed.

Joey's apology that Max is an "old man" brings a spasm of violence from
Max against both Joey and Sam. Energized by this execution of paternal and
manly authority, Max turns to Ruth more kindly: "You a mother?" (III, 59).

When he learns that she has three sons, his initial reply reflects his own insecurities: "All yours, Ted?" (III, 59). Then, in the presence of an image of his wife, Max invites the embraces of his returning son.

This familial bond extends into act 2, which begins with Max, Sam, Lenny, and Teddy lighting cigars in masculine contentment, an image mocked throughout the play. As Bernard Dukore has explained (Dukore, "A Woman's Place," 113) for all their bullying, the men in this house lack masculinity. Max devotes himself to womanly activities: cooking and tucking the boys into bed. He even talks about his own pangs of childbirth. Lenny runs away when Ruth offers herself to him, and Sam is virtually sexless, while Joey later fails to go "the whole hog" with Ruth, and Teddy retreats behind an intellectual barrier.

Perhaps Ruth understands her strength from the start; after all, she has experience with all kinds of men. Thus she is never out of control. Here she compliments Max on the quality of the meal, and Max is equally gracious about her coffee. The warmth of the moment inspires Max into a tribute to Jessie: "Mind you, she taught those boys everything they know. She taught them all the morality they know" (III, 61–62). He adds that she had a "heart of gold" (III, 62), a stereotypical quality of fictional prostitutes. The nature of the family business is emphasized when Max recalls negotiating with "a top-class group of butchers with continental connections" (III, 62), a meeting so promising that he pledged an assortment of garish gifts for his wife:

> [. . .] and I said to her Jessie, I think our ship is going to come home, I'm going to treat you to a couple of items, I'm going to buy you a dress in pale corded blue silk, heavily encrusted in pearls, and for casual wear, a pair of pantaloons in lilac flowered taffeta. Then I gave her a drop of cherry brandy.   (III, 62)

The phrase "for casual wear" suggests an advertisement, as if Max were promoting a new style of clothes rather than offering a present to Jessie. Here is the side of Max that charmingly invited women to work for him, as he "sold them a line" before he literally "sold them." He adds: "I remember the boys came down, in their pyjamas, all their hair shining, their faces pink, it was before they started shaving, and they knelt down at our feet, Jessie's and mine. I tell you it was like Christmas" (III, 62). Max takes comfort in the image of the boys before they were old enough to be rivals. We cannot know whether the incident ever happened, but we understand that the memory is intended to intimate to Ruth the potential warmth of the family into which she has stepped. In contrast to the brutality we have seen, the recollection is comically jarring. Ruth, however, does not allow Max to maintain this illusion, as she characteristically brushes aside surface action and language by posing a question that brings everyone down to the primitive level: "What happened to the group of butchers?" (III, 63). Max confirms that "They turned out to be a bunch of criminals like everyone else" (III, 63).

This rambling reflects the romantic side of Max's personality, his affection for women and family. His next lengthy speech reveals his vulnerability, as he elaborates on his struggles to maintain such luxury: "A crippled family, three bastard sons, a slutbitch of a wife—don't talk to me about the pain of childbirth—I suffered the pain, I've still got the pangs—when I give a little cough my back collapses—and here I've got a lazy idle bugger of a brother won't even get to work on time" (III, 63). Max is infuriated over diminishing power. All he can do is insult Sam: "You'd bend over for half a dollar on Blackfriars Bridge" (III, 64). His insinuation of homosexuality is an attempt to make Sam even less of a man than Max.

Therefore Max turns to Teddy and Ruth and casually asks why Teddy never told the family he had married. Teddy's excuse is amusingly lame: "You were busy at the time. I didn't want to bother you" (III, 65). But we soon understand Teddy's real reasons. Now Max begins to concentrate on Ruth herself, as he offers his "blessing" (III, 65) on the marriage. Ruth, however, starts to exert her own will: "I'm sure Teddy's very happy . . . to know that you're pleased with me. (*Pause.*) I think he wondered whether you would be pleased with me" (III, 65). Here is Ruth's invitation. In retrospect we suspect Teddy was afraid that his family would be all too pleased with her, but Ruth solicits further examination. Anticipating the course of events, Teddy rises to defend his way of life:

> She's a great help to me over there. She's a wonderful wife and mother. She's a very popular woman. She's got lots of friends. It's a great life, at the University . . . you know . . . it's a very good life. We've got a lovely house . . . we've got all . . . we've got everything we want. It's a very stimulating environment. (III, 66)

The passage is another in which the literal meaning is undercut by the tone and rhythm with which the words are uttered. Teddy's lack of passion implies first that his life is the opposite of what he claims and second that Ruth is probably unhappy. Therefore Teddy's statement is a plea that Ruth be allowed to remain with him. Moreover, the suggestion that Ruth is so popular on campus has ironic undertones about the reasons why.

The family, though, is relentless. When Max inquires whether the children miss their mother, Teddy insists that they do, until Lenny coolly reminds Teddy: "Your cigar's gone out" (III, 67). The line implies that Teddy has lost his power. Teddy responds in kind, but Lenny retorts in a different vein, encroaching on Teddy's territory, his area of expertise: "Do you detect a certain logical incoherence in the central affirmations of Christian theism?" (III, 67). The incongruency of such a question from Lenny is comic, but his intention is serious. Richard Dutton suggests that the question reflects Lenny's cynicism: "It is the absence of faith, the absence of such certainties, in respect of the lost mother, Jessie, which lies at the heart of the odd behaviour within the family" (Dutton, 132). Something more important is also happening. Lenny is also challenging Teddy's way of life, indeed, his right to Ruth. Teddy, however, sidesteps the issue: "That question doesn't fall within my province" (III, 67). Lenny pursues further, posing hypotheses on the nature of reality: "Well, for instance, take a table. Philosophically speaking. What is it?" (III, 68). All Teddy can respond is "A table" (III, 68). He has surrendered, unwilling to hold his intellectual ground, and his retreat is an acknowledgment that he will not fight in any other arena. Thus when Max and Joey join in Lenny's derision, Ruth takes on her own cause:

> Look at me. I . . . move my leg. That's all it is. But I wear . . . underwear . . . which moves with me. . . . it . . . captures your attention. Perhaps you misinterpret. The action is simple. It's a leg . . . moving. My lips move. Why don't you restrict . . . your observations to that? Perhaps the fact that they move is more significant . . . than the words which come through them. You must bear that . . . possibility . . . in mind.   (III, 68–69)

On one level she suggests that language itself, the words an individual uses, may not be the key to that individual's meaning. On another level, she insinuates that although she is married to Teddy and to all appearances committed to him, legalities do not constrain her. Her instincts, her very nature as a woman, are more important. Thus she is free to act as she wants.

After Teddy stands, surrendering by relinquishing his place in the family unit, Ruth reveals that she was "born quite near here" (III, 69). Therefore this homecoming is not only Teddy's; it is also hers. We may speculate that she was the instigator of the trip, for she describes her life in America as lifeless, twice invoking the image of insects, an image that suggests contempt for Teddy and his colleagues. (III, 69). Max, Joey, and Lenny then exit, satisfied that Ruth is eager to stay.

Left alone with his wife, Teddy virtually begs her to return to America with him, but his urgings are laughably inadequate: "The fall semester will be starting soon" (III, 71). Not even the mention of her sons moves Ruth. She queries whether Teddy finds his home dirty, and at first he denies that hypothesis, but then he picks up the theme: "Here, there's nowhere to bathe, except the swimming bath down the road. You know what it's like? It's like a urinal. A filthy urinal!" (III, 71). His disparagement of the London environment is nullified when Ruth calmly postulates about Venice: "But if I'd been a nurse in the Italian campaign I would have been there before" (III, 71). This echo of Lenny's remark in act 1 puzzles Teddy, but clarifies for us Ruth's identification with Lenny.

As if on cue Lenny returns, and Ruth becomes subtly assertive. She asks Lenny's opinion about her shoes, then complains that she cannot obtain ones she wants in America (III, 72). The underlying meaning of her query is whether Lenny supplies proper clothes for his women. Lenny reassures Ruth that he has recently bought a woman a particularly stylish hat. In turn she details her experience as a photographic model who worked in the nude. The passages suggest her confidence in her identity as a woman, an impression reinforced by the shocking scene that follows.

As Teddy comes downstairs with the luggage, he is eager to leave, but Lenny asks Ruth for a dance. Then Joey takes over, and before long he and Ruth embrace on the sofa. Max enters to watch, commenting to Teddy with hilarious detachment: "Listen, you think I don't know why you didn't tell me you were married? I know why. You were ashamed. You thought I'd be annoyed because you married a woman beneath you" (III, 75). Here Pinter makes a visual pun, for Joey is at the moment on top of Ruth. Meanwhile Max extols her attributes: "A mother of three. You've made a happy woman out of her. It's something to be proud of. I mean, we're talking about a woman of quality. We're talking about a woman of feeling" (III, 76). The outlandishness of the action on stage, in juxtaposition with the double entendre of Max's commentary, is set off even more by Teddy's silence, which amounts to complicity.

When the audition is over, Ruth stands. She has proven herself by demonstrating her skill at manipulating men sexually. Furthermore, these men need her for emotional, financial, and sexual reasons. Therefore the power in the house, and in the business, is hers, and she knows so. When she orders food and drink, her manner is terse, her sentences short: "Well, get it" (III, 76). Then: "What's this glass? I can't drink out of this. Haven't you got a tumbler?" (III, 76). Throughout the play requests and demands for sustenance have added to the parodic elements, an ironic mockery of a nurturing instinct. By ordering such materials for herself, Ruth accepts her place within the tribal organization, and her severe tone reaffirms that she expects compliance.

Her gradual disengagement from Teddy continues when she asks: "Has your family read your critical works?" (III, 77). Teddy takes the moment to offer a defense: "There's no point in my sending you my works. You'd be lost. It's nothing to do with the question of intelligence. It's a way of being able to look at the world. It's a question of how far you can operate on things and not in things" (III, 77). The analysis is Teddy's justification for his passivity. He refuses to participate in the family ways, to fight for his own wife, or to stand for any principles:

> Might do you good . . . have a look at them . . . how certain people can maintain . . . intellectual equilibrium. Intellectual equilibrium. You're just objects. You just . . . move about. I can observe it. I can see what you do. It's the same as I do. But lost in it. You won't get me being . . . I won't be lost in it.   (III, 78)

This statement has greater implications. John Elsom has suggested: "Teddy is someone who has lost his roots, both by being educated in a manner which has lost him an accent and a strange, rough sub-culture and by becoming too 'rational': he distrusts and fears the instinctive emotions which surround him" (Elsom, 110). True, Teddy fears those instincts, but he also suffers from a lack of feeling that turns him into an outcast from his family, and in no way may he be judged heroic. One implication is that Teddy's intellectual sophistication, the product of his undergraduate and graduate education, may also have removed him from normal human emotions. He uses philosophical training not to understand life, but to set himself apart from it.

Indeed, he may be seen as a peculiar collaborator, willingly surrendering to what he recognizes as the evil surrounding him. Michael Craig, who played Teddy when the original Royal Shakespeare Company production came to the United States in 1967, has commented: "He's an awful man, Teddy. He's rationalized his aggressions, but underneath he's Eichmann" (quoted in Hewes, 56).

A possible reason for Teddy's ostracism is offered by Sam in the next brief scene, which takes place that evening. Sam inquires whether Teddy knew MacGregor, and again we wonder if Teddy, so different from his brothers, is MacGregor's offspring. Sam also claims that Teddy was Jessie's favorite, again opening the possibility that Teddy was special because he had a different father.

The pair are joined by Lenny, who has come to look for his cheese roll. When he learns that Teddy has taken it, Lenny is taken aback: "Barefaced audacity. (*Pause.*) What led you to be so . . . vindictive against your own brother? I'm bowled over" (III, 80). We, however, see Teddy's action as a feeble gesture of revenge. The family has appropriated Teddy's wife; he retaliates by consuming Lenny's cheese roll.

In response Lenny embarks on a lengthy speech, ostensibly modest in tone, but in fact mocking Teddy's insecurity and inefficacy: "And so when you at length return to us, we do expect a bit of grace, a bit of je ne sais quoi, a bit of generosity of mind, a bit of liberality of spirit, to reassure us" (III, 81). Teddy can only mumble a monosyllabic reply.

As his family's behavior becomes more outrageous, Teddy's retreat becomes more vicious. When Joey returns after a session with Ruth, without having gone "the whole hog," Teddy replies: "Perhaps he hasn't got the right touch" (III, 82). He sits silently through an extended narrative by Lenny and Joey about how they raped two girls near Wormwood Scrubs. Finally Max returns: "Where's the whore? Still in bed? She'll make us all animals" (III, 84). Max intuitively understands the truth. Amazingly, Teddy is the one who explains: "He had her up there for two hours and he didn't go the whole hog" (III, 84). The disparity between the cultured professor and the crude slang, the bizarre situation of a man reporting on the sexual escapades of his wife, make this line one of the most comically grotesque in a play full of dark wit. Equally funny is Max's paternal solicitude: "My Joey? She did that to my boy?" (III, 84). He seems genuinely worried that Joey has suffered psychic wounds.

Max also may be revealing his antagonism toward Ruth and the control that she as a woman has over male sexual fulfillment. He blames her for taunting his son, but Max is also jealous of her power. He inquires whether Teddy has received similar treatment, but Teddy refuses to take the question or lower himself to the family's level. All he answers is "No" (III, 85), an ironic echo of Ruth's earlier replies to him.

At last Max articulates what has been apparent for some time: "You know something? Perhaps it's not a bad idea to have a woman in the home. Perhaps it's a good thing. Who knows? Maybe we should keep her" (III, 85). From this point on the proposition is debated with a dispassion both horrifying and hilarious. Perhaps the most revolting aspect is Teddy's refusal to be perturbed: "The best thing for her is to come home with me, Dad. Really. We're married, you know" (III, 86). Although Teddy pretends to be superior to his family, in his own way he sinks lower than they do, for he refuses to acknowledge the outrage taking place. We think again of his philosophical background, which apparently permits, even encourages, such detachment.

The comedy grows blacker as the men weigh details of their scheme, financial, domestic, and sexual arrangements, all the while feigning deeper feelings. As Max says to Lenny: "But I think you're concentrating too much on the economic considerations. There are other considerations. There are the human considerations. You understand what I mean? There are the human considerations. Don't forget them" (III, 87). Lenny answers politely: "I won't" (III, 87), but Max's generous tone drops at once: "Well don't" (III, 87). That shift reflects the conflict within Max. He is talking about a maternal figure, but he is also talking about a whore. His polite, even reverential, manner is appropriate to one, but not to the other. Moreover, to Max, Lenny is a filial figure, to be treated kindly, but also a sexual competitor, who must be dispatched if Max is to maintain status and power. In one moment Max speaks from his identity as father; in the next he speaks from his instinct as sexual predator.

After Teddy calmly refuses to put "anything in the kitty" (III, 87) to support Ruth's staying in London, Lenny suggests that they "put her on the game" (III, 88). The details are weighed with brazen coldness, as Lenny suggests that Teddy might be able to provide an international clientele: "No, what I mean, Teddy, you must know lots of professors, heads of departments, men like that. They pop over here for a week at the Savoy, they need somewhere they can go to have a nice quiet poke. And of course you'd be in a position to give them inside information" (III, 90). The obscene double meaning of "inside information" aside, Lenny's scheme suggests that sex is merely a biological process, divorced from emotion. Underlying this entire play is a vision of human beings as no more than beasts, creatures of instinct and sensual pleasure, for whom morality and societal standards are shackles to be discarded.

Ironically, when Ruth enters, Teddy is the one who proffers the scheme: "Ruth . . . the family have invited you to stay, for a little while longer. As a . . . as a kind of guest. If you like the idea I don't mind. We can manage very easily at home . . . until you come back" (III, 91). Perhaps Teddy is trying to outdo his family, to be even colder and more vicious than they. Max, meanwhile, overflows with compliments: "But you . . . Ruth . . . you're not only lovely and beautiful, but you're kin. You're kith. You belong here" (III, 91). Such flattery means nothing to Ruth, who seizes the proposal and treats it as no more than a cold financial arrangement. The longer she speaks, the more "ruthless" she becomes: "All aspects of the agreement and conditions of employment would have to be clarified to our mutual satisfaction before we finalized the contract" (III, 93). If Lenny and the family regard sex as business, Ruth sees it as a source of strength. Not only is she capable of fulfilling male needs; Ruth also understands that these needs are biologically compelling. Hence, in her identity as a woman, with her sexual instincts under control, Ruth has power that the men cannot challenge. Therefore she dictates the terms.

Sam suddenly shouts: "MacGregor had Jessie in the back of my cab as I drove them along" (III, 94). This outcry is his way of protesting, but he is also telling Teddy that neither one of them belongs as part of the family. Under the strain of rebellion Sam collapses. James Hollis explains Sam's crisis: "His dilemma is to find himself in a group that obeys the laws of the blood, laws which are preconscious, presocietal" (Hollis, 105). Sam is completely unlike Max, his brother, just as Teddy is unlike his two brothers. Perhaps both were born outside the family unit, and that is why Sam feels his kinship with Teddy: "Teddy lacks the moral courage to oppose his family, and Sam lacks the physical strength" (Hollis, 105). Max dismisses the prone body: "A diseased imagination" (III, 94). Perhaps he does not want to acknowledge the possibility of dubious paternity. A more likely explanation is offered by Hugh Nelson:

Poor Sam's carefully concealed fact, his delayed exposition, his last-minute message, is of no importance and never was of any importance. The characters have made their decisions on the basis of what each wishes to remember of the past, what each wants to see in the present, what each needs, desires, and fears. That decision is inevitable, irrevocable.   (Nelson, 152)

After humorously formal partings, Teddy prepares to leave. Again, his coldness and refusal to acknowledge what has happened may be rebellion, but it is in no way heroic. Ruth's final line to him, though, is puzzling. She calls him "Eddie," then adds: "Don't become a stranger" (III, 96). The nickname is a sign of affection, so perhaps she wants him to know that despite her actions she does have feelings for him. The line also intimates that on a certain level they have remained strangers, and that this parting has been inevitable. John Warner goes so far as to claim that the split is actually a positive action: "In rejecting her husband, whose province is words, and in staying with his family, she seeks not simply promiscuous pleasure, but greater existential wholeness" (Warner, 351). This assertion is echoed by Sakellaridou, who derides the "inadequacy of the males in *The Homecoming*..." because of "their tendency to see themselves as fragments of a whole, in contrast to Ruth's struggle for wholeness and integration" (Sakellaridou, 115).

The vague satisfactions of "existential wholeness" or "wholeness and integration," however, are irrelevant, as subsequent action implies. With Teddy gone, Ruth assumes her place at the center of the family. As Pinter himself has said, "At the end of the play she's in possession of a certain kind of freedom" (Hewes, 57). Joey kneels at her chair, and she pats his head, as if he were a pet. Lenny stands to the side, watching, but doing nothing more. Max, however, seems finally to grasp her strength. As he stammers and collapses, he cries that he will be able to satisfy and that he will demand to be satisfied. His protests are both demands and pleas, attempts at male dominance and wails of childlike helplessness.

Elin Diamond suggests that "in this unstable stage tableau, no one can be called victorious" (Diamond, *Pinter's Comic Play*, 157). Yet as Ruth sits on her parody of a throne, we recognize that even though she will play the roles of wife, mother, whore, and mistress that fulfill all the desires these men have, as well as those that other men will bring her, she is the ultimate figure of authority in this home. Even Almansi and Henderson, who largely dismiss realistic interpretations, suggest that *The Homecoming* can be seen as a powerful plea for feminine and feminist independence (Almansi and Henderson, 69). Steven Gale also supports this perspective: "She fulfills different needs for the various men in her new family in order to fulfill her own needs" (Gale, *Butter's Going Up*, 155).

Most critics, however, see Ruth's triumph as tainted. In Richard Schechner's words, the play is "a probe of the dark male attitudes toward the 'mother-whore' and the equally compelling female desire to play this double role" (Schechner, 183). The key word is "compelling." As Hugh Nelson has written:

> . . . what we see in the attitudes and responses of the characters and in their
> relationships to each other is a reality which is prehistoric and primitive, a world
> where appetite reigns . . . Beneath the stated values of the play, there is a total
> absence of values, a void which is filled by the human family's animal struggle
> to survive and perpetuate itself.   (Nelson, 161)

Irving Wardle devoted an entire article to what he calls "the territorial struggle": "What we see, in other words, is a ritualized tournament in which the two instincts of sexual desire and territorial aspiration fight it out under the scrutiny of an emasculated winner on the sidelines. There is no doubt that territory is the winner" (Wardle, 44).

John Russell Taylor articulates the nature of Ruth's triumph very effectively:

> In the battle for power, naturally the body wins out over the mind; the
> weapons of Teddy and Sam are too feeble to wound Max, Lenny, or Joey. But
> then men, even when ruled entirely by their bodies, by instinct, are no match
> for women who make no practical distinction between body and mind, but
> think-act or act-think in one dissoluble process; it is Ruth therefore who must
> finally dominate Max, Lenny, and Joey, just as they have necessarily domi-
> nated Teddy and Sam.   (Taylor, "Pinter's Game," 63)

This interpretation is supported by the perspective of Thomas Postlewait, who places Pinter's work in relation to the family dramas of Ibsen. Postlewait discusses how in Ibsen's plays

. . . passion and power are linked dangerously, threatening the stability of family life. This convention of characterization (while not necessarily the truest image of women) suggests that passionate desires, deeply incarnate and hidden from view, drive women to seek power over men by means of sexual allurement.   (Postlewait, 203–204)

He correctly concludes that Pinter, too, uses such a power/passion convention in *The Homecoming*: "He is, in fact, making explicit a theme and mode of characterization in Ibsen's plays: the female body as a commodity in a conflict between power and desire" (Postlewait, 211–212).

The most crucial aspect of *The Homecoming* is that underlying the play is a psychological realism, a depiction of forces that drive men and women toward authority and acceptance, and sexual and emotional fulfillment. To bring these forces to light, Pinter dramatizes that without the constraints of conventional morality, certain elemental aspects of human nature inevitably manifest themselves. Ruth, the woman, ends up dominant because of her capacity to deny emotion and to fulfill the divergent, yet complementary, needs of various males. Nonetheless, she has agreed to play roles determined by these men, and thus the parameters of her superiority are sharply defined. From another perspective, she has turned to the family to find a new, satisfying identity; simultaneously she will provide another dimension of meaning and order for the men around her.

One of Max's final lines is a cry of fear and warning: "She won't . . . be adaptable!" (III, 97). But Max misreads the nature of Ruth's power. She is, in fact, completely adaptable, able to do whatever is necessary to maintain authority. Such is the manner of her survival in the jungle of the family, in the eternal tension between the male and female divisions of our species, here presented with uncompromising savagery and wit.

5

Tea Party
The Basement

First produced on television in the mid-sixties and transferred to the stage a few years later, these plays are often performed together. They offer intriguing variations on the battle between men and women for power within relationships, as well as explore the interior of the mind, dramatizing how imagination, memory, and desire shape our drives and reactions. The structure of the works reflects such thematic development, as Barbara Kreps indicates:

> As Pinter's plays have moved farther and farther away from anything like stage naturalism, there has been a corresponding increase in the plays' overt self-consciousness, through structure and images which call attention to the fact that they *are* structures and images. (Kreps, 57)

Thus the objective of territorial struggle remains the same, but the boundaries are expanded. The plays also reflect how instinct appears in a variety of forms to dominate human thought and action.

TEA PARTY

Tea Party was originally a short story, told in first person from Disson's perspective. Vestiges of that form still dominate the script, for almost all that happens is seen through Disson's eyes, while the central conflicts occur within his mind and lead to the breakdown of his mental capacities. Here, too, sexual and social forces contend for authority and space, but what makes this battle especially intriguing is that Disson is both the lone combatant and the lone victim of the struggle. The play is essentially realistic, but it has a peculiar texture, for throughout the work we observe only his distortion of ideas, words, and images. Thus the battle is between Disson and the social and sexual forces around him; the battlefield is Disson's mind.

At the start of the play, as Disson interviews Wendy for a secretarial job, some of his desires are apparent: "You've had quite a bit of experience" (*Tea Party*, III, 103). From this point on almost every line, no matter how innocent Disson means it to be, takes on sexual overtones. Furthermore, because Disson's firm manufactures bidets, a product that embarrasses him, innocuous phrases like "area of work" and "discharging it" sound suggestive. He also is self-conscious when describing the responsibilities of the job: "A very private secretary, in fact. And a good deal of responsibility would undoubtedly devolve upon you" (III, 104). The word "devolve" seems formal; yet at the same time it sounds curiously intimate. Furthermore, Pinter's focus on Wendy's crossing her legs increases the eroticism of the occasion, particularly in Disson's mind.

The last element in the scene to intensify Disson's excitement is Wendy's revelation about advances made upon her by her previous boss. Disson's understated expression of sympathy, "What a monster" (III, 105), in conjunction with his probing questions, suggests that he understands the other man very well, and that similar desires lurk within Disson himself.

In the next scene the contrast between Disson's urges and the family environment he is about to join by marriage becomes evident. The dialogue is stiff, and Diana's reaction to the news that Disley will be unable to serve as best man reflects her coolness: "How infuriating" (III, 107). In fact, this absence allows the war taking place within Disson to surface, for he seems to feel himself unwelcome. As he explains his disappointment at Disley's absence and Willy's intention to present the appropriate toasts, Disson cannot disguise his insecurity about the marriage altogether: "Yes, but look . . . I mean, thanks, very much . . . but the fact is . . . that you don't know me, do you? I mean we've only just met. Disley knows me well, that's the thing you see" (III, 107). He feels himself constricted, even trapped.

Postponement seems the logical step, but the next scene is the wedding dinner, where events confirm Disson's doubt. First Willy pays tribute to "our father": "A man whose business was the State's, a man eternally active, his one great solace from the busy world would be to sit for hours on end at a time watching his beloved daughter ply her needle" (III, 108). The image of a worldly, upper-class gentleman of sophistication contrasts sharply with Disson's vision of himself. Willy proceeds to another toast, ostensibly in praise of Disson, but the tribute turns into a paean to Diana: "Par excellence as a woman with a needle, beyond excellence as a woman of taste, discernment, sensibility and imagination" (III, 109). The baroque sentence structure contributes to Disson's fear that he is marrying out of his class. As a joke Willy adds: "An excellent swimmer who, in all probability, has the beating of her husband in the two hundred metres breast stroke" (III, 109). Even Disson's manhood is under attack.

The dialogue, too, suggests that inert feelings exist beneath the surface of this marriage. For instance, Willy attempts to cheer his sister: "You have married a good man. He will make you happy" (III, 109). The words themselves are innocent, but if we imagine them heard through the distortions of Disson's mind, they communicate a lack of passion that makes Disson's subsequent desire for Wendy that much more compelling—thus the conflicting attitudes about women in Disson. As Arnold Hinchliffe has commented, the play "is very much about the nature of woman, represented by the secretary Wendy . . . and the wife Diana (significantly named after the goddess of chastity)" (Hinchliffe, "Mr. Pinter's Belinda," 176). What Hinchliffe omits is that this dual nature is in Disson's mind, not in the women themselves. As we have seen, however, Disson's split vision is common to several men in Pinter's plays.

This effect is reinforced first by the brief scene in the hotel room, where Diana and Disson speak unseen. Disson's repetition of "Are you happy?" (III, 110) and the lifeless responses it earns suggests a sterile relationship. Disson's unhappiness is also reflected in his brief exchange with his two teenage sons.

When they attempt to call him "sir," he resists, feeling himself the target of upper-class affectation. His self-consciousness is aggravated further when he must supply his aristocratic, yet apparently insolvent, brother-in-law with a job. As happens so often in Pinter's works, a character who speaks at great length does so for self-justification, and here Disson's roundabout explanations of company procedures suggest his self-consciousness at holding a pedestrian career. First he establishes his own character: "I'm a thorough man. I like things to be done and done well. I don't like dithering. I don't like indulgence. I don't like self-doubt. I don't like fuzziness. I like clarity" (III, 113). Disson's claims of order are a confession that he fears loss of control, that he holds to procedure to prevent inner collapse: "Nothing is more sterile or lamentable than the man content to live within himself. I've always made it my business to be on the most direct possible terms with the members of my staff and the body of my business associates" (III, 113). The unintentional irony of his words strikes us on a least two levels. First, Disson's life is utterly cold and devoid of feeling, his isolation manifested at every turn. Second, his concern with "the body" of his associates is soon to take on a meaning different from that which he intends. His insecurity grows when Willy proposes that Diana, his sister, also be his secretary. Disson's strained reaction implies that he feels his territory and independence threatened: "But she doesn't need to work. Why should she want to work?" (III, 114). Then in the next scene Wendy announces: "Mr. Disson does not want to be disturbed until 3:30." With virtually every line, Disson feels his economic and personal power, his authority over his own life, even his very identity, under attack.

His paranoia is dramatized effectively in the scene between his wife and sons. They speak of him kindly, but the dialogue has a strange intonation, almost inhuman in its lack of passion. For instance, John's final comment, seemingly benign, should be read in an ironic tone, so as to take on a sinister aspect: "Well, it really all depends on how good you are at making adjustments. We're very good at making adjustments, aren't we, Tom?" (III, 115). Here Disson enters. They smile at him, but he looks around in panic, like a trapped animal.

His repressed feelings surface in the next scene, when he suggests that Wendy sit on his desk. With her emphasis on her high heels and her detailed plan for standing on the edge of her chair, the sequence has an erotic quality.

Disson tries to dismiss her hesitancy: "Look, get up or stay down. Make up your mind" (III, 117), but his emphatic denial instead reinforces that he is battling to control his lust for her.

Disson's breakdown begins in the table tennis match, when he thinks he sees two balls served instead of one. This awkwardness takes him to Disley for an examination, and we realize that Disson's psychological difficulties are taking the form of physical debilitation. His pain recalls that of Rose in *The Room* and Edward in *A Slight Ache*, for all three suffer visual trauma stemming from emotional distress. Their blindness is symbolic of vulnerability, their inability to find security. That Disley can find nothing physically wrong with Disson's eyes is further proof of the psychological war taking place within him, the result of an attempt at territorial defense complicated by sexual desire.

Disson attempts to diffuse the situation at dinner, gently insinuating that he would prefer Diana not to be at work, but she is insistent: "Because by being your employee I can help further your interests, our interests. That's what I want to do. And so does Willy, don't you?" (III, 123). The ease of Disson's conversation here is in contrast to the clipped sentences in the next scene, when Wendy solicits compliments about her new dress. First she boldly chastises him for sitting in her chair and denies being late, then suddenly flirts girlishly: "I've put on my new dress" (III, 123). Like so many of Pinter's other female characters, Wendy can switch roles instantly, and that capacity unnerves Disson. His brief phrases reflect his repressed urges, which nonetheless emerge in his subsequent quarrel with his sons. He is attempting to teach them manual skills, to instruct them in his way of life, so to speak, but they have no aptitude and would prefer to complete their paper on the Middle Ages, the sort of scholarship about which Disson, whose formal education is limited, knows nothing. The shot of the saw near Tom's fingers reflects latent violence beneath Disson's surface. When Tom complains that his fingers were nearly cut off, Disson shouts in self-defense: "You didn't hold the wood still!" (III, 125). Even his fundamental skills are slipping, reflecting his fading powers.

In the next scene his desperation and erotic desires are played out for us. Wendy wraps her chiffon around his aching eyes to provide comfort, but simultaneously she arouses him. As Disson touches her, she begins to usurp his power, answering the phone and speaking for him. His impotence is emphasized in his hearing what he imagines to be loveplay between Willy and Wendy, although when the door opens Diana looks down at him, while Wendy sits and takes dictation from Willy. The psychological and physical aspects of his breakdown now appear simultaneously, as Disson verbally assaults Diana: "Don't speak to me like that. How dare you speak to me like that. I'll knock your teeth out" (III, 127). What is most intriguing, however, is that no one but Disson himself causes this breakdown. His mind persecutes him, and he is helpless to defend himself against his own drives.

In the next scene these take the form of a game. Disson's absorption with Wendy's body, reflected in the television production in a close-up shot of her buttocks, is transformed into the mock football match played with the lighter. The tone changes, though, when she genuinely invites him to come after her: "Come on, tackle me! Get the ball! Fight for the ball!" (III, 130). Once she fights back and Disson is no longer the aggressor, he collapses, and all he can do is retreat to formal dialogue: "Have you everything you want? Are your working conditions satisfactory?" (III, 130). His desire for Wendy and the social decorum that stifles his attraction for her leave him helpless. This condition is mocked in the next scene, as Disson lies in bed with Diana. He reads a life of Napoleon, perhaps in search of inspiration for leadership. Meanwhile Disson seeks reassurance: "You've got enough money, haven't you? I mean, you have sufficient money to see you through, for all you want?" (III, 131). She responds affirmatively, but the blandness of her tone increases the pressure that we feel in Disson's next encounter with Wendy. He is dictating a letter, when the television screen suddenly goes black. Now Disson is temporarily blind, as his psychological frustration manifests itself in physical weakness. Meanwhile we hear only Wendy's voice, as she coquettishly taunts Disson: "You're playing one of your games, Mr. Disson. You're being naughty again" (III, 132). Once more the combination of flirting and mothering, familiar from other Pinter plays, reflects male vulnerability before the multiplicity of sexual roles a woman can play.

Disley assures Disson that nothing is wrong with his eyes, but the recollection of the wedding and Willy's reading of Disley's speech lead to the outburst in the next scene, as Disson hears Willy's recollections about himself and Diana at their childhood home. Disson tries to interject recollections of his own: "What are you whispering about? Do you think I don't hear? Think I don't see? I've got my memories, too. Long before this" (III, 134). The outrage earns no response. Finally Disson's self-doubt emerges publicly when he bluntly asks Diana: "Why did you marry me?" (III, 135). He seeks reinforcement, but his refusal to take her at her word prompts Willy to inquire as to Disson's state. When Willy genially inquires whether he has offended Disson, Disson not only denies this possibility, but offers to take on Willy as a partner. One reason for this gesture is for Disson to soothe his conscience at his anger. He may also want to deflect Wendy's attention away from himself.

The brief scene between Wendy and Diana concentrates our attention on the biological desires within the women themselves. First Diana speaks with her husband's secretary: "I understand your last employer touched your body . . . rather too much" (III, 136). Perhaps Diana, sensing that her husband is attracted to Wendy, seeks to understand more about her. When Disson enters, however, their conversation communicates to him that the women are conspiring, an impression confirmed by their silence at his departure. This alliance is not presented as a conscious banding together. Instead the two women are dramatized as instinctively seeking each other's support.

From this point Disson's breakdown proceeds more quickly. First he collapses during a table tennis match with Willy. Following a loveless interlude with his parents, he continues his passive-aggressive game with Wendy, alternating between insults, demands, and resignation. She expresses her pleasure in this contest, which borders on sadomasochism: "I always feel like kissing you when you've got that on round your eyes. Do you know that? Because you're all in the dark" (III, 139). The last line epitomizes Disson's dilemma. He is not only literally, but also figuratively in the dark, unable to grasp what forces plague him. Yet he is compelled to seek both Wendy and Diana, and also compelled to act with them the way he does. As Disley says to him in the next scene: "This'll keep you in the dark, all right. Also lend pressure to your temples. Is that what you want?" (III, 140). Disson's reply: "That's it. That's what I want" (III, 140). Helpless to deal with his drives, Disson is eager to submit to them and find some perverse fulfillment, but he remains frustrated, as Burghardt notes:

> Sexually Disson commits himself to two diametrically opposed women. Diana loves him because of his strength, his vision, his self image. Wendy is attracted to him only when he is blindfolded and helpless. He cannot be both and these sexual relations tear him apart. (Burghardt, 387)

The fragmented structure of the remainder of the script mirrors the disorder in Disson's mind. Snatches of dialogue and glimpses of figures are intertwined, interrupted by bland conversation at the tea party. The subsequent shot, however, is from Disson's point of view, and reveals the animal-like fear he holds: *"Figures mouthing silently, in conspiratorial posture, seemingly whispering together"* (III, 143). This sense continues as conversation is interspliced with silent shots.

The images become blatantly sexual when Willy embraces both Diana and Wendy. When Wendy receives an invitation to Spain, her imminent departure suggests that part of Disson's world is collapsing. Now we can assume that the action is in Disson's mind, as Wendy and Diana lie beside each other on a table, head to toe. After a shoe drops, Disson's mind seems to explode, and he falls to the floor. The others try to help, but he can only stare blindly ahead as Diana calls to him. Simon Trussler suggests that at this point Disson "has become a reluctant version of Teddy in *The Homecoming*, incapable of movement as he watches the supposed seduction of his women" (Trussler, 142).

Throughout *Tea Party* Disson's desires are a combination of domination and submission, of financial superiority complicated by social and sexual inferiority. When he is unable to find happiness at any level, with either woman, he collapses. As the victim of drives that demand to be satisfied, yet are impossible to satisfy, he suffers loss of home and job, and therefore loss of power and identity.

THE BASEMENT

Although, as indicated, *The Basement* has been performed on stage, it retains its strongest effect in its original medium, television, for no play of Pinter's is more a part of the mind. Indeed, at many points we cannot be certain whether what we see is reality, memory, or imagination, nor can we be sure whose mind is being dramatized. Thus the fluidity of the script is hampered by the bounds of stage reality.

Still, despite the ambiguous plot, a familiar theme pervades: the conflict between the biological and the emotional. In addition, the script presents a battle for power and territory, although who is winning, or how, or why, is less definable.

As the play opens, Law sits in his apartment, giggling while reading a Persian love manual *"with illustrations"* (*The Basement*, III, 152). The implication is that Law desires what he cannot find in life, and thus he seeks fulfillment through fantasy. He is visited by Stott, apparently an old friend, although the circumstances of their earlier relationship are never clarified. Law acts paternally toward Stott, offering towels and allowing him to share Law's home. Yet Stott remains impassive, hardly greeting Law and not bothering to explain the unexpected arrival; the only reason provided is that "I'm looking for a place" (III, 154). Thus a struggle for territory unfolds. It is complicated, however, by Stott's bringing Jane with him, for at once Law finds himself a stranger in his own home, as Jane refuses his dry towel but accepts Stott's wet one. She also begins to establish possession: "What a splendid room" (III, 155). Within moments she and Stott have stripped off their clothing and taken to Law's bed, where they make love while he returns to his manual. The boldness of the scene and the situation of two people making love while a third sits nearby struggling to maintain dignity is comic, but laughter does not disguise the usurpation.

Here the puzzle grows thicker. First the scene shifts from winter to summer and from inside to outside. Then Law and Jane talk about a third man, an old friend of Law's: "He has a connexion with the French aristocracy. He was educated in France. Speaks French fluently, of course. Have you read his French translations?" (III, 158). The other man is likely Stott, although Law and Jane observe Stott next in a cave, sleeping. Is this scene a fantasy of Law's? Or a memory? Because the scene follows a shot of Law reading and creating images, we can assume that the tableau takes place in Law's mind, an effect Kreps clarifies:

> For the crucial thing about the play is not Law's definition in space, but his definition in time. And an important corollary of Law's personal time structure is that, as it is he who peoples his loneliness, he—like the artist—creates, defines, and destroys relationships as a private act of imagination.   (Kreps, 53)

The action returns to Law's apartment, where Jane and Stott lie in bed and Law rests on the floor. He and Jane exchange glances. Is Jane flirting with him? Perhaps she and Law were once lovers, only to have Stott take Law's place. Indeed, Law and Stott are likely in competition for Jane, and she is ultimately to choose between them. Stott then begins to dismantle Law's apartment, while Jane cooks. Soon we learn that Jane, in Stott's words, "comes from a rather splendid family, actually" (III, 160). Both she and Stott seem to be wealthy, while Law is not of their class. Should the play be regarded, then, as a class struggle as well as a sexual one? Why does Stott talk about Jane to Law, who may have known her first, as is suggested in the next scene? Here Jane and Law make love, but although Jane is enthusiastic, Law, as his name implies, fears discovery. Is Law a figure of conformity, who feels the threat of Stott's presence? Perhaps the entire series of images is a battle of instincts taking place within Law.

Perhaps the answer that best resolves most of these questions is that the story is not linear, a structure that suggests that life itself is not one single direct progression, but a sequence of events that stimulates a whirl of memories and fantasies. These may occur, then fade, then return, all uncontrollably. Nevertheless, a theme emerges: the struggle between two men for possession of a woman. Indeed, the alternation between winter and summer suggests a struggle that follows the cycle of seasons, while the movement from the natural, almost primitive, beach to the artificial environment of the room implies a war between instinctual desire and restraint imposed by society.

In the next scene the room is furnished in a second style, exotic Scandinavian decor that represents Stott's taste, or at least Law's version of Stott's taste. Then Law tries to dissuade Stott from an arrangement whereby all three would live together. Moreover, Law refers to the Town Council's disapproval, an excuse that again implies his fear of anything outside the bounds of propriety. Thus here, too, instinct battles rationality, as the primitive forces Stott seeks to unleash are stifled by Law's boundaries of civilization. On the other hand, if we view the play as taking place in Law's own imagination, we may surmise that the forces within the man himself are in conflict.

We also note Jane's passivity. In a scene in an empty bar, she sits by silently as the two men recall their early friendship. The banter, however, ends with a note of competition, as Stott suggests that Law is no longer unbeatable at squash (III, 162). The implication is that Stott's claim on Jane is also open to attack. Jane may thus be viewed as the prize in a competition fought by the two males. In fact, in the next episode she drops a scarf to signal the start of a race. Law runs and falls, while Stott watches him. If this sequence is all part of Law's memory or imagination, he may be picturing himself as foolishly chasing after Jane, a target beyond him.

In the next several scenes these tensions are magnified. Stott and Jane are embracing when Law bursts in with a recording of Debussy. Later Stott pursues Jane, trying to touch her breast, but she breaks away; in the next scene Law resumes the chase. Then Jane is shown whispering confidentially to Law, recalling happier days together and urging him to get rid of Stott. Where does her loyalty lie? Or, rather, where does Law imagine her loyalty lies? Or, rather, where does he fantasize that her loyalty should lie? Whether the scenes are real or imagined, the thematic import is the changeableness of Jane's affection and the battle between the two men for possession of her.

The less civilized battle of this play is intensified when Law and Stott are pictured alone. Law whispers to a resting Stott, working hypnotically to turn away Stott's affections:

> She betrays you. She betrays you. She has no loyalty. After all you've done for her. Shown her the world. Given her faith. You've been deluded. She's a savage. A viper. She sullies this room. She dirties this room. All this beautiful furniture. This beautiful Scandinavian furniture. She dirties it. She sullies this room. (III, 166)

No matter whether we regard this scene as realistic or imaginary, the theme is familiar: Jane is dramatized as inherently untrustworthy, and her unfaithfulness breaks down the relationship between the two men. Christopher Hudgins perceptively places this theme in the context of Pinter's oeuvre: "At the same time, as in so many Pinter triangles, there is the veiled suggestion that Law would really like to get rid of Jane and to reestablish the close relationship with Stott he remembers so nostalgically" (Hudgins, 79). Here, too, as in other Pinter plays, a woman's ability to play different parts for different men is viewed as inherent in her nature and a crucial aspect of her capacity for dominance.

At the end of The Basement the struggle for survival is portrayed in more graphic terms. First Law and Jane muse over what may be a dying Stott. Immediately afterward they are described as "snuffling each other like animals" (III, 167). As if too repellent to maintain, this image is cut off by a suddenly awakened Stott, who opens and closes the curtains on yet another arrangement in Law's room, this one Italian. Is this scene Law's fantasy about using Stott's own technique to commit revenge against Stott? Possibly, but civilized combat quickly descends into more elemental forms. First Law and Stott take part in a game of marbles, which grows more brutal with Jane on the sidelines cheering the ensuing destruction. In Law's mind the two men still compete for her affection.

A marble strikes Law's head, a blow that probably represents Law's image of how Stott might react to losing Jane. Law collapses, then awakens to a scene of sheer primitivism. The room is bare, and as the two men engage in a death struggle, Jane, in a mockery of domesticity, pours milk on the side. Here is the struggle for survival and possession of the female in the rawest form yet, since Stott's aggression draws out Law's innate violence. Yet this picture is only a reflection of deeper forces: "The implication is that it is the woman who brings in the tone of animality since, archetypally, she is associated with the world of instincts and the unconscious rather than with the intellect and the conscious mind" (Sakellaridou, 58).

The final tableau reverses the beginning of the play, an ironic commentary on all that has proceeded. Nevertheless, other questions loom. Is this ending an actual reversal of roles? Or is Law imagining triumph over Stott, who is now inside and reading, as Law was at the start? The question cannot be resolved. But the battle for survival, the pageant of warring drives and instincts, remains the essential fabric of the play:

> It is the longing for being in the uppermost position which acts as the impulse in the figures' mutual relations, blossoming into scenes of duel, battle, violence, where mime and gesture take first importance of the intentional evasion of speech.   (Rosador, 204)

In addition, the cinematic presentation is essential to the play's impact:

> The departure from realism, the seemingly strange shifts in perspective without warning or traditional exposition, successfully present a character's mental responses to the reality around him, picturing repressed hostility, the musings of wish fulfillment, warped perception, and subconscious drives and fears.   (Hudgins, 81)

In *The Basement* the battle for survival and possession takes place almost exclusively in the realm of the mind. Nonetheless, the elements of Law's struggle are, in one form or another, at the core of all the plays considered here. In this work a male struggles for self-definition and identity within a relationship. That identity, however, can be achieved only through dominance of a female and subjugation or elimination of a male rival. As in the rest of his plays, Pinter dramatizes both conflicts as instinctual aspects of human nature. He also suggests how much of gender conflict is intellectual. Power does not mean simply physical domination, but also psychological control, first of oneself, then of one's rivals. We think of Flora in *A Slight Ache*, Bill in *The Collection*, and Ruth in *The Homecoming*. Characters who master their own desires, who are at ease with their own natures, are the ones who dominate territory and other inhabitants of that territory.

6

Landscape
Silence

From their premiere performances on stage in 1969, these two works have often been presented together, for in style and theme they are intimately related. They are the most Beckettian of Pinter's works: spare in plot and setting, but richly lyrical. Yet here, too, familiar themes emerge, though in uniquely evocative forms. These plays dramatize struggles for authority and identity, but the competition is oblique, the victories and defeats shadowy. The most important element is the contrasting natures of men and women and their differing attitudes, values, and desires.

Both plays are contemporaneous with a sketch of Pinter's called *Night*, which was first produced as part of the revue *Mixed Doubles* in April 1969. Although the piece is almost incidental, it is worth exploration, for it reflects motifs found in other Pinter plays. The script depicts the conversation of two characters, designated "Man" and "Woman," both in their forties, who reminisce over coffee. Their memories diverge, however, in telling ways.

The two agree that they met at a party given by the Doughtys, but from there matters are less certain. The Woman is preoccupied with romantic images: "You took my face in your hands, standing by the railings. You were very gentle, you were very caring" (*Night*, III, 224). She hears a child crying and is distracted, but the Man is more concerned with sensual recollections:

"We stopped on a bridge. I stood behind you. I put my hand under your coat, onto your waist. You felt my hand on you" (III, 225).

Gradually the Man's memories become more sexual: "I put my hands under your sweater, I undid your brassiere, I felt your breast" (III, 225). At this suggestion the Woman seems to recoil: "Another night perhaps. Another girl" (III, 225). Perhaps the brazenness of the picture spoils her idyllic memory, and she resists its being soiled. On the other hand, like the characters in *The Collection*, the Man and the Woman probably remember what they want to remember, what images give them comfort and security. This playlet thus anticipates several plays to follow (*Landscape, Silence, Old Times*) where recollection itself is the subject. In these works the shape of the present is determined by memories that characters are compelled to recall, by memories that characters choose to recall, and by memories that characters claim to recall.

Under such circumstances memory itself can be a battleground on which struggles for power are carried out. In this sketch, however, the Man and the Woman join in marital contentment, as at the end they put aside their differences. The Man acknowledges a moment they shared: "And you remembered your bottom against railings and men holding your hands and men looking into your eyes" (III, 226). He offers to complement her recollections by admitting that she was desired by men other than he. She welcomes that suggestion: "And they said I will adore you always" (III, 226). The Man completes the image: "Saying I will adore you always" (III, 226). He allows the Woman to retain her sense of herself as eternally desirable, while he acknowledges that he accepts that need and loves her anyway. In Adler's words:

> But the husband accepts and supports the memory on the wife's terms, acceding to her subjective truth. By understanding that her emotional needs differ from his own, the husband can participate imaginatively and creatively in the memory world of his wife.   (Adler, "Pinter's *Night*," 464)

Such empathy in this short work produces a warmth between male and female that is virtually singular to Pinter's plays. The competition for power in the relationship is abandoned, as the Man happily surrenders to the Woman's vision. In subsequent works memories do not blend; instead they clash, creating psychological competition in which the stakes are identity, security, and power.

LANDSCAPE

Memory is at the heart of this play, but it is not memory that comforts. Instead a struggle between male and female values takes place in the realm of the mind, although the participants are not precisely antagonists. Rather they are mutual victims, prisoners of their own natures and of fundamental differences in need and desire.

The structure of the play reflects this dichotomy, as Pinter dispenses with almost all traditional trappings of drama. Although the setting is the kitchen of a country house, the two actors hardly interact with the furniture or background. Instead they sit apart, speaking essentially monologues, as their past and present unfold. What gives the play its impact is first how the two stories intertwine but remain apart, as we try to distinguish truth from illusion and memory from fantasy; and second, how the nature of the woman keeps her detached from her husband, how her memories and hopes reflect a spirit of love and romance that clashes poetically with his earthier desires.

The play begins with Beth's recollections, the gentle memories of a time on the beach. The beauty of the images suggests her affinity with natural phenomena, as if by her nature as a woman she is part of the cycle of life, an aspect emphasized by her hope to have children with the man at her side. We also sense her reliving these images as part of a desire to resist age. The identity of the man in her narrative remains vague, but from the start we are conscious of her frustration with him: "I walked back over the sand. He had turned. Toes under sand, head buried in his arms" (*Landscape*, III, 178).

Duff, whose name suggests his comparative crudeness, shatters the tone with his first words: "The dog's gone. I didn't tell you" (III, 178). He is involved only with the present, and his concerns remain mundane. A few sentences later he speaks of children: "With some youngsters. I didn't know them" (III, 178). To him they are anonymous bodies, while to Beth they are a symbol of life.

Yet as Lucina Gabbard points out, the two characters have important qualities in common: "The play presents a picture of present loneliness and past longings. Two unfulfilled souls live out their emptiness—together but isolated" (Gabbard, 221). She adds that both begin their recollections with images of water: Beth speaking of the sea, Duff of the pond. Gabbard, whose book is a psychoanalytical approach to Pinter's works, here suggests that such memories imply a longing "for the love and security they once had at birth" (Gabbard, 221).

In his stage directions Pinter notes that *"Duff refers normally to Beth, but does not appear to hear her voice"* (III, 176), while *"Beth never looks at Duff, and does not appear to hear his voice"* (III, 176). The implication is that Duff attempts to reach Beth but does not care or notice whether she responds, while Beth is so involved in her own feelings that Duff's presence is superfluous to her. Duff's isolation is portrayed as weakness, Beth's as inner strength.

Before long their monologues intersect. Duff says: "There was a man and woman, under the trees, on the other side of the pond. I didn't feel like getting wet. I stayed where I was" (III, 179). He resists any bond. Beth, on the other hand, searches for that attachment: "They all held my arm lightly, as I stepped out of the car, or out of the door, or down the steps. Without exception. If they touched the back of my neck, or my hand, it was done so lightly. Without exception. With one exception" (III, 180). The theme of touching recurs throughout the play, suggesting that Beth seeks an intimacy different from the gratification enjoyed by Duff. Such desire coincides with the estimate of many biologists about one of the crucial differences in sexual response between men and women: that women react to a variety of sensual stimulations, in particular tactile sensation (Moir and Jessel, 107). Beth's yearnings reflect such a desire for intimacy apart from the sexual act itself.

The aesthetic qualities of Beth's reminiscences have suggested to Elizabeth Sakellaridou that:

> Pinter highlights the contrast between the artist and the common man by stressing the polarity of Beth's femininity and Duff's masculinity. Viewed from this angle the play puts aside the sexual division and deals underneath with two basic human attitudes, the romantic and illusionistic on the one hand and the unemotional realistic on the other.   (Sakellaridou, 151)

This point is partially correct; we are conscious of a split between the romantic and the realistic. Sakellaridou fails to note, however, that throughout Pinter's plays women have a more acute aesthetic, even romantic, sense, while men lose themselves amid prosaic elements of life. Thus the division in this play does not mark a blurring of genders, as Sakellaridou claims, but an emphasis on the distinctive qualities of each gender.

In the midst of such delicacy, Duff appears ever more coarse: "Mind you, there was a lot of shit all over the place, all along the paths, by the pond. Dogshit, duckshit . . . all kinds of shit . . . " (III, 180). The clash of tones is comic; yet its implication is more sad than funny. These two individuals function on different planes. The comedy is that they must live together and try to nourish each other. The tragedy is that they are incapable of doing so.

Beth's memory grows more intimate. First, however, she clarifies that she has changed little from the loving woman of her own memory: "I could stand now. I could be the same. I dress differently, but I am beautiful" (III, 180). Duff, however, fails to hear her: "You should have a walk with me one day down to the pond, bring some bread. There's nothing to stop you" (III, 180). He remains trapped in the present, unwilling or unable to come to grips with the failures and disappointments, as well as the joys, of Beth's past. Meanwhile her images on the beach become more sensual, but she does not dwell on the purely sexual. What matters to her most is the intimacy of the occasion, the sharing of quietude with the man at her side.

The recollections of the two speakers intersect again when they speak of the bar, although once more the two invoke disparate words and ideas. Beth recalls wondering how the man might order and thinks about his voice (III, 183). Duff offers cruder details: "This beer is piss, he said. Undrinkable. There's nothing wrong with the beer, I said" (III, 183). At this point we speculate whether Duff could have been the man on the beach with Beth. Does she harbor memories of the way he was, a gentle man coarsened by time and events? Duff's description of an unpleasant row in the bar, and Beth's quick discarding of the newcomer, suggest that she disliked his manner and sought refuge in the sensual delight of the sand and the water at what appears to be her most sensitive spot, the back of her neck.

Another possibility arises with the mention of Mr. Sykes, in whose home Beth and Duff worked as servants. Not only did they work there; they may also have become the owners, as Duff indicates that they took control: "I thought of inviting one or two people I know from the village in here for a bit of a drink once or twice, but I decided against it" (III, 185). Now we ponder whether the man from Beth's memories might be Mr. Sykes. Beth still recalls happy memories and laughter on the beach with the nameless man, but Duff's reference to her success in running the house implies a special warmth between Beth and the owner: "He trusted you, to run his house, to keep the house up to the mark, no panic" (III, 186). Duff seems aware of the bond, but not of its depth, for when he recalls returning from a trip with Mr. Sykes, he remembers that Beth "stopped still" (III, 187). Apparently Duff assumed that her emotional turmoil was caused by her not seeing him for so long, whereas we assume that she missed Mr. Sykes.

Instead Duff chooses that moment to confess his infidelity, and he recalls that Beth did not cry. Her stoicism may be the result of her desire to hold on to her husband, or perhaps a sign of unconcern, a reflection that the real object of her desire was a man other than Duff, possibly Mr. Sykes. On the other hand, Beth earlier recalled the man commenting on her sad manner: "My gravity, he said. I was so grave, attending to the flowers" (III, 180-181). Duff has similar memories: "I was thinking . . . when you were young . . . you didn't laugh much. You were . . . grave" (III, 186). Here the man in Beth's memory is likely Duff, so that we may assume that he has changed profoundly over the years.

Despite his brusqueness, Duff seems aware of the affection Sykes had for Beth. Duff claims that the owner was "a gloomy bugger" (III, 188), but that the man did give Beth a "nice blue dress" (III, 188). The depth of the recollections that follow reinforces that Beth misses such attention: "He moved in the sand and put his arm around me" (III, 188). Duff tries to fill the void: "Do you like me to talk to you? (*Pause.*) Do you like me to tell you all the things I've been doing?" (III, 188-189). Beth remains apart: "And cuddled me" (III, 189). We feel both characters maneuvering for security, seeking authority by recreating memories that subdue the other's energies and needs.

Duff's nature, however, does not preclude his capacity for affection. He recalls: "I was very gentle to you. I was kind to you, that day. I knew you'd had a shock, so I was gentle with you. I held your arm on the way back to the pool. You put your hands on my face and kissed me" (III, 190). Yet Duff speaks of a pond, while Beth speaks of the ocean, a force more passionate and dramatic, and the difference underscores the clash of memories and values. So does Duff's casual dismissal of the woman with whom he had an affair: "The girl herself I considered unimportant. I didn't think it necessary to go into details. I decided against it" (III, 190). On the other hand, the deception Beth recalls, whether it actually occurred or not, was a key part of her life. Another possibility is that Beth seeks some combination of gentleness and aggression, the sensitivity of Sykes united with the energy of Duff.

Perhaps Beth wants the two men and cannot be satisfied with one or the other. She needs the qualities of both in one individual, and the impossibility of that joy precludes her happiness.

Gradually the monologues return to the present. Beth dwells on the fragility of time: "Of course when I'm older, I won't be the same as I am, I won't be what I am, my skirts, my long legs, I'll be older, I won't be the same" (III, 192). She understands the ephemerality of human life and love. Duff, meanwhile, with little sense of time, maintains blinders: "At least now . . . at least now, I can walk down to the pub in peace and up to the pond in peace, with no-one to nag the shit out of me" (III, 192). While Beth struggles to recapture those lost moments, Duff fails to see their significance: "That's what matters, anyway. We're together. That's what matters" (III, 192). His insistence on the immediate, his denial of the value of the past, reflects what Pinter portrays as masculine callousness, Duff's inability to feel passion as deeply as does his wife.

The two monologues now diverge sharply, as Beth flows deeper into reverie and Duff becomes preoccupied with an argument over the quality and manufacture of beer. The clash of voices is both comic and moving, as Duff's words become increasingly onomatopoeic: "bung," "bunghole," "spile the bung" (III, 193). After a long silence Duff's tone changes, perhaps reflecting resignation: "I never saw your face. You were standing by the windows" (III, 195). The rest of this speech seems to be his recollection of an attempt to grow closer to her, but apparently she resisted, as she does at this moment by talking about perspective:

> I remembered always, in drawing, the basic principles of shadow and light. Objects intercepting the light cast shadows. Shadow is deprivation of light. The shape of the shadow is determined by that of the object. But not always. Not always directly. Sometimes it is only indirectly affected by it. Sometimes the cause of the shadow cannot be found. (III, 195–196)

Simon Trussler suggests that this speech is "a statement of the play's determining sensibility—its feeling for the shapes of the shadows thrown by the past, or sometimes by no discernable cause at all" (Trussler, 161). This evaluation may be applied to much of Pinter's work, especially those plays that focus on the influence of memory.

In growing anger Duff broods about her past actions, now tied to her present distance: "It's bullshit. Standing in an empty hall banging a bloody gong. There's no one to listen. No one'll hear. There's not a bloody soul in the house. Except me" (III, 196). Mr. Sykes either departed or died, Beth mourned him, and her preoccupation with him left Duff enraged. He had hoped she would turn to him. Instead she remained preoccupied, and Duff claims that in fury he wanted to or perhaps tried to rape her: "I would have had you in front of the dog, like a man, in the hall, on the stone, banging the gong, mind you, don't get the scissors up your arse, or the thimble . . . " (III, 197). Eigo comments:

> At no point in the play do the characters so diverge as they do in their final pronouncements. Language is a primary reason. Duff's one-syllable words and hard consonants beat out a staccato rhythm while Beth's longer words and liquid consonants flow melifluously [sic]. The language reflects the subject matter and underscores the couple's separation.   (Eigo, 182)

Whether Duff actually attacked Beth is uncertain. What we can conjecture is that this attack, or the fantasy of an attack, or even the threat of an attack, permanently severed the relationship between Duff and Beth. It left them asunder: living together, but isolated spiritually. When Duff found himself unable to conquer Beth emotionally, he tried to dominate her physically, to find his security in her subjugation. His failure was caused primarily by his inability to satisfy her myriad needs and desires.

Thus the final few lines of the play, all Beth's, are shattering. In memory she returns once more to the beach, recalling the same sensual detail in which she has reveled throughout the play. The simple last line is the most overwhelming: "Oh my true love I said" (III, 198). It is a confession that she no longer loves Duff. If we assume, as seems likely, that the man on the beach was Mr. Sykes, then Beth's final words imply that she never loved Duff, that he was always subordinate in her life.

Gabbard effectively articulates the impact of *Landscape*: "The whole play becomes a concretization of alienation and incompatibility highlighted by each character's final memory images—his of debasement and hers of gentleness" (Gabbard, 221). *Landscape* also dramatizes the different instincts of men and women about love. Duff is well meaning but blunt and crass, and for that reason can never fulfill Beth's needs. Although his violence and energies are passionate, his capacity to give love is far more shallow. Beth, however, as a woman, has more profound desires but is also capable of giving and is eager to give much more in return. The man with whom she might have shared happiness was, because of circumstances, part of her life for but a brief time. Now that he is gone, she is sustained only by his memory.

SILENCE

The obvious link between Landscape and Silence is their minimalist structure: intersecting monologues in which memory, reality, and imagination blend cryptically. A more subtle point of comparison is their dramatization of the differing needs and attitudes of men and women. In Silence that gap becomes powerfully evident.

As in Landscape, the emotional isolation of the characters is reflected in the setting, in which three areas are distinguished, each with a chair. Here Pinter does not offer even the semblance of a realistic background. Rumsey, described as a man of forty, begins with a recollection of a stroll with a girl in gray. The images are gentle and intimate:

> I tell her my life's thoughts, clouds racing. She looks up at me or listens looking down. She stops in midsentence, my sentence to look up at me. Sometimes her hand has slipped from mine, her arm loosened, she walks slightly apart, dog barks.   (Silence, III, 201)

He seems fulfilled by the moment. But Ellen's first comments indicate that although she was part of Rumsey's memory, the experience was not as complete for her:

> He listens to me. I tell him what I know. We walk by the dogs. Sometimes the wind is so high he does not hear me. I lead him to a tree, clasp closely to him and whisper to him, wind going, dogs stop and he hears me.

> But the other hears me.   (III, 201–202)

Ellen insinuates that the two men she remembers from her girlhood in the country played different parts in her life. Each "heard" her, and each was vital to her. Indeed, the rest of the play suggests that as a woman, Ellen, like Flora in *A Slight Ache* or Stella in *The Collection*, has desires that are more complex than those of the men around her, that one man alone may not be able to fulfill all her yearnings. When Bates speaks, we hear a new tone that communicates precisely what he offers that Rumsey does, or did, not: "Caught a bus to the town. Crowds. Lights round the market, rain and stinking. Showed her the bumping lights" (III, 202). A few lines later he adds: "Brought her into my place, my cousin runs it. Undressed her, placed my hand" (III, 202).

Bates's language is brusque. He is a man of the city, and he hustles the woman in question (Ellen, possibly) back to his place. The implication is that Bates is less refined, more elemental. Rumsey is less demanding, more reflective. Each treats Ellen differently, but each nonetheless gives her something the other cannot. As Ellen says: "There are two. I turn to them and speak. I look them in their eyes. I kiss them there and say, I look away to smile, and touch them as I turn" (III, 203). In her memory or imagination both men are simultaneously part of her life. In reality, we suspect, such satisfaction was never achieved.

The men, too, have needs. Rumsey seems content in the tranquility of his country home: "Pleasant alone and watching the folding light. My animals are quiet. My heart never bangs" (III, 203). That his heart never "bangs" implies an absence of deep feeling and a desire for a passion that his solitary life cannot provide. Bates, too, has regrets. In a speech that seems to come from him at an older age, he broods: "I'm at my last gasp with this unendurable racket. I kicked open the door and stood before them. Someone called me Grandad and told me to button it. It's they should button it. Were I young . . . " (III, 203). Perhaps the man who was once spry enough to handle the excitement of the city is now too old to compete. He contemplates altering his path: "If I changed my life, perhaps, and lived deliberately at night, and slept in the day. But what exactly would I do? What can be meant by living in the dark?" (III, 204). As James Hollis points out, this rumination has important implications:

> What can be meant by living in the dark is the metaphysical question that characterizes the entire play, even, the entire Pinter corpus. If we changed our lives

and lived deliberately in the face of darkness, what exactly would we do; what would
be the consequences, the hopes entertained? Bates may be raising the right question
after all and, however uncertain the answer, raising the right kind of question may
well be better than not knowing what the question is.   (Hollis, 115)

The two views presented by Rumsey and Bates imply that no single pattern
of life can completely satisfy a man, just as Ellen's lines imply that no one
man can completely offer all that a woman wants. These needs also have
another side: the result of the inevitable passage of time. Ellen hints at its
influence when she mentions visiting an old woman. During this sojourn
Ellen claims that she, too, is old: "I'm old, I tell her, my youth was somewhere
else, anyway I don't remember" (III, 204). The events that seemed so
important, the brief moments of sensuality and emotional coupling, fade with
time. From this point on we wonder about the precision of Ellen's remem-
brances. If details of her life blur, how much does she recollect accurately?
How much does she create to soothe herself? Versions of this question might
be asked about virtually all Pinter's characters: Do they desire space or
authority, or do they seek love or physical pleasure? When they relate details
of their lives, when they try to put the past into perspective, how much of
what we hear is truth and how much fantasy?

The brief interlude that follows seems to be the moment when Bates
invites Ellen to his cousin's place, but in terse lines she refuses. Thus we ask
whether Bates's memory of the night is tainted, or whether his earlier
narrative was hope or illusion.

This uncertainty is followed by two brief excerpts, one each by Rumsey
and Bates. Both speeches suggest that without a woman, probably Ellen, the
men are painfully lonely. This need reflects male vulnerability, as Pinter
dramatizes it, and the particular strength of women. Again, although this
play, like *Landscape*, does not focus on a specific struggle for power, a battle
for survival is taking place. Like many women from Pinter's plays, Ellen has
an inner fortitude, while the two men, outwardly stronger, are inwardly
wounded. Indeed, Bates's comments about the birds emphasize their finding
comfort and refuge, whereas he has been unable to do so (III, 208). Rumsey,
too, is isolated: "Sometimes I see people. They walk towards me, no, not so,
walk in my direction, but never reaching me, turning left, or disappearing,
and then reappearing, to disappear into the wood" (III, 208).

This sentiment is contrasted presently by the brief phrases of Ellen and Rumsey, recreating what seems to have been a moment of mutual delight in the country. Their love is undercut by the next tableau, in which passion becomes mere memory. Ellen and Rumsey are apparently much older, and Rumsey implies that Ellen has not visited his home since she was a little girl (III, 209). Evidently she grew up in the country, then left him. Perhaps she fell in love with someone else, most likely Bates. Ellen may have needed more than Rumsey, alone in the deserted farm neighborhood, could provide. Possibly their dialogue implies the inevitable disappointment that accompanies any decision we make; we cannot have all that we want from life. Ellen left Rumsey behind. She may have found some other satisfactions without him, but she also never knew again the particular pleasures he offered.

Such seems to be the import of Ellen's next reminiscence, one evidently from her old age: "Is it me? Am I silent or speaking? How can I know? Can I know such things? No-one has ever told me. I need to be told things. I seem to be old. Am I old now? No-one will tell me. I must find a person to tell me these things" (III, 211). Bates, too, is lonely, as he reveals in the speech immediately following. This juxtaposition suggests the inevitable isolation of old age, that whatever choices we make, whatever affections we choose to share, life leaves us ultimately alone, searching our memory, trying to answer questions that are beyond solution. A. R. Braunmuller makes a key point: "All three seek a recreative power in memory: it releases them from the moment's demands, and it permits, or seems to permit, the mind to discover relation and control" (Braunmuller, "Pinter's *Silence*," 126). In other words, the characters use memory to salvage the present.

After Ellen's discourse on old age, she recalls a curiously passionless sexual moment (III, 211) when a man had asked permission to kiss her. We cannot be sure how old she was or how old she remembers herself being, but the disembodied tone communicates that the moment was unpleasant and may account for her inability to surrender herself to passion later on. Immediately following, the two men offer bits of enigmatic dialogue about their inability to communicate with Ellen. The lines hint that in her own way Ellen was beyond the realm of either man. Both failed to understand all the feelings inside her, and neither was able to fulfill all that she needed. The brief exchange that follows reveals that at one time Rumsey understood that Ellen wanted more than he could provide, and he urged her to find an appropriate young man. She resisted, but we glean from the rest of the play that she did seek someone else, who turned out to be Bates. Together they moved away from the country to live in the city. Yet the relationship was ultimately unsatisfying. As Bates says: "Sleep? Tender love? It's of no importance" (III, 213). Although he and Ellen shared a life, they did not happily share their lives. The result has left Ellen in a vacuum:

> After my work each day I walk back through people, but I don't notice them. I'm not in a dream or anything of that sort. On the contrary. I'm quite wide awake to the world around me [. . .] Yes, I remember. But I'm never sure that what I remember is of to-day or of yesterday or of a long time ago. (III, 214)

The last line is essential to Pinter's oeuvre, both theatrically and thematically. It also echoes one of the most poignant lines from Samuel Beckett's *Waiting for Godot*, uttered by the blind Pozzo in act 2: "I don't remember having met anyone yesterday. But to-morrow I won't remember having met anyone to-day" (Beckett, *Waiting for Godot*, 56A–57). Both playwrights are preoccupied with the uncertainty of our knowledge of the past, as here Ellen asks whether her memory is reliable, or whether it is as much imagination or dream.

From this point on the play breaks down into fragments, many of which echo previous lines. The effect, as Esslin has suggested, is "the way in which the last moments of awareness of a dying person might remain suspended in limbo for ever, echoing on and on through eternity, while gradually losing their intensity but unable ever to fade away completely" (Esslin, *Pinter the Playwright*, 186). The series of recollections also evokes, as Gabbard points out, Beckett's *Krapp's Last Tape*, in which the title character dwells on one moment of lost love, as he floats in a boat on a lake: "I lay down across her with my face in her breasts and my hand on her. We lay there without moving. But under us all moved, and moved us, gently, up and down, and from side to side" (Beckett, *Krapp's Last Tape*, 23). Krapp, too, can only look back at the past with resignation: "Perhaps my best years are gone. When there was a chance of happiness. But I wouldn't want them back. Not with the fire in me now. No, I wouldn't want them back" (Beckett, *Krapp's Last Tape*, 28). Like the characters in *Silence*, he must rely on memory to create a bearable present.

The structure of Ellen's reactions to both men suggests the complex nature of the women in Pinter's plays. Ellen was attracted both to Rumsey's bucolic, gentle manner and to the more aggressive nature of Bates. Her strength was her capacity to share with both men. The sadness of her life is that she had to choose one and deny herself the pleasure of the other. Nonetheless, we feel Ellen as the determining agent in this work, the active personality in the mutual struggle for identity and security, while the two men, each in his own way, live as a part of her.

7

Old Times

In *Butter's Going Up*, a study of Harold Pinter's works, Steven Gale twice refers to *The Homecoming* as Pinter's best play (Gale, *Butter's Going Up*, 136, 147). In a more recent essay, however, he confers that honor on *Old Times* (Gale, "Deadly Mind Games," 127). The revised judgment is understandable. *Old Times* has an elegance, a poetic grace, that belies the battle for affection, territory, and power that connects it with other Pinter plays. In addition, the struggle here takes on a special quality: *Old Times* is the dramatization of a labyrinthine system of memory images, some of which we understand to be factual, but many others of which may be created or purposefully distorted so that the speaker can assert his or her authority over the present. True, such tactics are part of every Pinter play. We think of Lenny's monologues in *The Homecoming*, or any of several narratives in *The Collection*, *The Birthday Party*, or *The Caretaker*. In *Old Times*, however, the tone is singular, as Stephen Martineau clarifies: "The strong difference and the added tension in *Old Times* is that the past becomes a competitive arena, a matter of life and death" (Martineau, 292).

The opening tableau establishes an atmosphere charged with doubt and contention. Deeley is *"slumped in armchair"* (*Old Times*, IV, 3), seemingly defeated even before the battle has begun. Kate is *"curled on a sofa"* (IV, 3), a position that suggests both repose and security. Finally Anna is *"standing at the window, looking out"* (IV, 3), as if emotionally and intellectually detached. She may also be seen as formulating plans, waiting for an opportunity to take control.

Furthermore, when the dialogue between Kate and Deeley starts, Anna remains in the background, a placement that also suggests multiple roles. She may be regarded as a constant presence for the speakers, as well as a more active force, biding time until the proper moment of invasion. On yet one more level she may be the source of contention between husband and wife. This combination of passive and aggressive behavior is the essence of Anna's tantalizing presence.

Kate's opening word, "Dark" (IV, 3), is at the thematic core of the play, suggesting the recesses of mind and memory that the characters probe. It will also be challenged by the play's final tableau, which is set in very bright light. Thus the progression seems to be from uncertainty to knowledge, but in fact this scheme is ironic, for at the end the characters and the audience are no more assured of the truth than at the start. According to this perspective, the play has a satiric edge that mocks the characters and their mutual attempts at manipulation, as well as a rueful tone that reflects the desolation of three people who struggle for home and identity in an environment that makes such claims difficult to achieve.

From the opening lines, Deeley is on the defensive, as he inquires about Kate's past relationship with Anna. These repeated attempts to clarify the bond the two women shared reveals his jealousy, his doubts about his wife's fidelity, and perhaps his fears about his masculinity.

Kate, on the other hand, revels in her position. She is vague about the meaning of "friend" (IV, 4), as if human relationships, including that between husband and wife, are beyond clarification. At first she refers to Anna as "my only friend" (IV, 5), then amends that to "my one and only" (IV, 5). The revised line is also the title of a musical comedy by Rodgers and Hart, and anticipates the exchanges of song lyrics between Deeley and Anna. Kate also mentions, as if by chance, that Anna used to "steal things" (IV, 6), then adds that some of the stolen articles include "Bits and pieces. Underwear" (IV, 6). The immediate implication is that the relationship between Anna and Kate was sexual, but a more important theme that emerges is that women, by their very nature, share an understanding of one another's physical and emotional needs that men cannot fathom and certainly cannot duplicate. In this respect both Kate and Anna remind us of Beth from *Landscape* and Ellen from *Silence*, whose sensibilities are so different from those of the men in their lives. Here, however, these contrasting sensibilities are turned into weapons. Kate has unique memories of Anna that always remain distinct from her relationship with Deeley. Consequently from the outset Kate implies that her womanliness isolates Deeley and that he is defeated even before Anna arrives. Furthermore, the contradictions Kate poses, claiming hardly to remember Anna, then providing all sorts of intimate details, establish ground rules for the competition to follow: memories and histories can be invented and used to assert authority over others.

That Kate understands and enjoys Deeley's submissive position is also clear, for she urges him to save his questions for Anna herself. When Deeley tries to challenge: "Do I have to ask her everything?" (IV, 9), Kate reverses the invitation: "Do you want me to ask your questions for you?" (IV, 9). No matter what Deeley does in response, he is lost. If he insists that Kate ask, then he concedes defeat. If he continues to ask questions himself, then offers those same questions to Anna, he remains acquiescent. Thus the false bravado of his reply: "No. Not at all" (IV, 9).

Deeley's next strategy is to ask about Anna's husband. When Deeley tries to confirm his existence, Kate is irritatingly vague: "Everyone's married" (IV, 9). Deeley asks several more times about him, but each time he is put off. Is Deeley trying to lessen Anna's appeal by reminding Kate that Anna no longer lives the carefree existence the two enjoyed when they were younger? If so, then Kate's last tactic before Anna's entrance is a countermaneuver, for Kate tantalizes Deeley with intimations about the possibly lesbian relationship between the two. When he repeats "You lived together?" (IV, 12), the repetition suggests both surprise and arousal. His last comment before Anna's appearance, "Anyway, none of this matters" (IV, 13), may express weakness, but it may also foreshadow Deeley's own scheme to insinuate himself into the past that Kate has established and that Anna will partially confirm.

Anna's first speech is a recollection of experiences shared with Kate, and thus is Anna's way of revivifying their relationship. As becomes clear, Anna's need to do so gives Kate the true power in this play, for it is she who is desired by both Deeley and Anna. In this respect Kate seems to have the strength of Ruth in *The Homecoming*, who, as the object of desire, achieves power.

As Elin Diamond points out, this triangle recalls the structure of Sartre's *No Exit* (*Huis Clos*, 1944), in which Inez, Estelle, and Garcin form three pairs, all bound by mutual need. Diamond also clarifies the similarity of the predicaments borne by the male character in each play, as their heterosexual affection faces competition from a lesbian (Diamond, 163–164). Here Anna quickly turns into Deeley's antagonist, and Kate settles back into her docile, yet oddly commanding, posture. Anna's first lines are a narrative about youthful escapades with Kate in London. The details immediately suggest the depth of their past intimacy: "[. . .] we sat hardly breathing with our coffee, heads bent, so as not to be seen, so as not to disturb, so as not to distract, and listened and listened to all those words [. . .]" (IV, 14). Deeley attempts to quash the importance of this memory by derogating the locale: "We rarely get to London" (IV, 14). But Kate affirms the significance of Anna's recollection: "Yes, I remember" (IV, 14). This simple line invites conflict between Deeley and Anna.

Yet two battles are carried on concurrently. One is between Anna and Deeley for possession of Kate. The other is between Kate and Deeley for supremacy within their marriage. This latter struggle is particularly intriguing:

> Both play by the same ground rules; each accepts that to remember an event makes it true. The conflict therefore centers upon a series of "old times," of superficially trivial reminiscences, and the characteristically Pinteresque ambiguities actually represent characters' conflicting attempts to rearrange the past to suit their own ends. (Hughes, 470)

Such competition begins almost from the moment Anna moves down into the light. After commenting on the desolation of Kate and Deeley's home, she uses the word "lest" (IV, 15), which surprises Deeley. Here is the first of several instances where Kate's vocabulary or sentence structure takes him aback, emphasizing his alienation from Anna and her relationship with Kate. Anna then hints at her own loneliness: "Sometimes I walk to the sea. There aren't many people. It's a long beach" (IV, 16). Then, out of nowhere, she comments: "You have a wonderful casserole" (IV, 16). The remark confounds Deeley, but Anna immediately clarifies: "I mean wife. So sorry. A wonderful wife" (IV, 16). Anna knows precisely how to upset Deeley, and here is the first occasion when she does so. When Anna denies Deeley's earlier conjecture about Anna's being a vegetarian (IV, 17), we realize that all statements of fact are up for grabs. Battle lines are drawn, soon to be erased and then redrawn.

The war begins subtly when Deeley and Anna begin to reflect on Kate's preferences. Anna asserts that Kate "was always a dreamer" (IV, 19), to which Deeley replies: "She likes taking long walks. All that. You know. Raincoat on. Off down the lane, hands deep in pockets. All that kind of thing" (IV, 20). His speech is meant to communicate that he understands Kate's present wants, as well as that Kate no longer needs to dream: she is satisfied with the life he provides. But his choppy phrases lack passion, and Anna's failure to reply immediately undercuts his assertion.

Instead she retorts with a memory of her own: "Sometimes, walking, in the park, I'd say to her, you're dreaming, you're dreaming, wake up, what are you dreaming? and she'd look round at me, flicking her hair, and look at me as if I were part of her dream" (IV, 20–21). Anna takes Deeley's image of walking and turns it into a much more intimate experience. Whether this memory is accurate, or whether Anna is making up the thought, is irrelevant. Its conception suggests a poetry and depth of feeling within Anna that Deeley cannot match. Anna's use of "gaze" (IV, 22) is another example of her distinctive tone that leaves Deeley off balance.

Nonetheless, he continues to compete: "Lovely to look at, delightful to know" (IV, 22). The remark sparks a fascinating exchange of song lyrics that Deeley and Anna pretend are no more than recollections of happy memories. Nonetheless, the pattern has a hostile, even sinister, quality.

As Deeley and Anna duel, their choice of lines reveals their individual personalities and the nature of their attachment to Kate. First Deeley sings: "Blue moon, I see you standing alone . . . " (IV, 23). He distantly admires Kate. Anna, however, counters with: "The way you comb your hair . . . " (IV, 23), a more intimate observation. All Deeley can offer in response is the refrain of Anna's song: "Oh no they can't take that away from me . . . " (IV, 23). The line hints at desperation. Anna pushes harder: "Oh but you're lovely, with your smile so warm" (IV, 23). She shows her strength first by moving to a different song, then by focusing on a physical quality of Kate's. Deeley retreats to an impersonal claim of ownership: "I've got a woman crazy for me. She's funny that way" (IV, 23). The subsequent pause suggests that this line is a concession on Deeley's part.

When Anna resumes by singing a three-line stanza, Deeley's reply hints at a subsequent turn of events: "That I get a kick out of you?" (IV, 24). He may be suggesting not only that he is interested in maintaining possession of Kate, but also that he has, or perhaps at one time had, possession of Anna. The episode concludes with the exchange of verses from "These Foolish Things," in which the title line is followed by the unspoken "[. . .] remind me of you." That Deeley and Anna end up singing the same song implies that their competition grows more direct. At the end, after Anna matches him line for line, Deeley resigns: "They don't make them like that any more" (IV, 25). He acknowledges both his inability to find new lines with which to confront Anna, as well as his lack of imagination to recall or create images from the past to challenge Anna's claim to Kate.

Instead Deeley resorts to a lengthy memory of his own. He recalls attending a showing of the film *Odd Man Out* (the title alludes to Deeley's current predicament) and lasciviously talks of two usherettes in the foyer:

> [. . .] and one of them was stroking her breasts and the other one was saying "dirty bitch" and the one stroking her breasts was saying "mmnnn" with a very sensual relish and smiling at her fellow usherette, so I marched in on this excruciatingly hot summer afternoon in the middle of nowhere and watched Odd Man Out and thought Robert Newton was fantastic.   (IV, 25)

He implies that he interpreted the two usherettes as a sexual challenge and that his walking into the theater was evidence of a willingness to confront these two women. He was also attracted by the presence of the lone woman patron in the theater: "And there she was, very dim, very still, placed more or less I would say at the dead centre of the auditorium" (IV, 26). He admits his dislocation: "I was off centre and have remained so" (IV, 26). Still, his capacity to leave the theater, then pick up this single woman, who turns out to have been Kate, is Deeley's evidence that he originally had the courage to take her from the environment of the two usherettes: "So it was Robert Newton who brought us together, and it is only Robert Newton who can tear us apart" (IV, 26). Thus the direct challenge to Anna. Furthermore, the smuttiness of the story may be Deeley's injecting earthiness into the present situation, to corrupt Anna's poetic devotion to Kate and show instead his own more masculine affection.

Anna replies coolly about another actor in the film: "F. J. McCormick was good too" (IV, 26). She is still confident. Moments later Deeley presses his narrative: "And then at a slightly later stage our naked bodies met, hers cool, warm, highly agreeable, and I wondered what Robert Newton would think of this" (IV, 27). Anna, however, dismisses this image with a line at the core of the play, indeed, at the core of the creative strategy employed by characters throughout Pinter's plays: "There are some things one remembers even though they may never have happened. There are things I remember which may never have happened but as I recall them so they take place" (IV, 27–28). At this assertion Deeley can only exclaim *"What?"* (IV, 28), and Anna turns his story upside down by recalling a man she discovered in Kate's apartment. At first he was "all crumpled in the armchair" (IV, 28), as Deeley is now. Anna describes him as crying, then after Kate's rejection advancing towards Anna: "[. . .] but I would have absolutely nothing to do with him, nothing" (IV, 28). She thereby trumps Deeley's narrative about his sexual boldness. Furthermore, Anna's confidence in her ability to triumph in a contest of will grows:

> No, no, I'm quite wrong . . . he didn't move quickly . . . that's quite wrong . . . he moved . . . very slowly, the light was bad, and stopped. He stood in the centre of the room. He looked at us both, at our beds. Then he turned towards me. He approached my bed. He bent down over me. But I would have nothing to do with him, absolutely nothing. (IV, 28)

Earlier Deeley hinted that he and Anna might have been attracted to each other. Here Anna cuts off that possibility, confirming that as a man Deeley offers her nothing. Moreover, her blatant revising of the memory concedes that the story is fantasy, but so assured is she in her capacity to create pictures that outstrip Deeley's that she flaunts the fabrication. She even adds that the man lay across Kate's lap, but that in the morning he left: "It was as if he had never been" (IV, 29). The implication is that no male can ever truly matter to Kate. Meanwhile Deeley's series of questions aimed at ascertaining the man's identity confirms his vulnerability.

Throughout this episode Kate remains silent, a pose that in Pinter's works is almost always a manifestation of strength. Now she rejoins: "You talk about me as if I were dead" (IV, 30). She quietly mocks the subtle war being fought over for her affections. Deeley then reverts to his professional standing, recalling memories of himself as an art student, and how his skills and appreciation won Kate. Yet Anna is unimpressed by this claim as well. First she demonstrates once more her deeper understanding of Kate: "Some people throw a stone into a river to see if the water's too cold for jumping, others, a few others, will always wait for the ripples before they will jump" (IV, 32). The speech is nonsensical, but so unnerved is Deeley that he is desperate to grasp the hidden meaning: "Some people do *what*? (*To Kate.*) What did she say?" (IV, 32). The implication of Anna's short speech and the longer one that follows is that Kate, not Deeley, made the choice. Thus Deeley's masculine prerogative is mocked. Kate, too, notes that her interest in Deeley is not as strong as it might have been earlier: "I was interested once in the arts, but I can't remember now which ones they were" (IV, 33). She clarifies that Deeley's creative side, to which he has pointed as the source of his wife's love, is no longer stimulating, and the corollary implication is that neither is he.

In response Anna brings back her own artistic memories, in a speech that ends with the surprising mention of *Odd Man Out* (IV, 34). If, as she implies, she was present during that same showing of the movie, then she undercuts the importance of Deeley's earlier narrative. Thus Deeley resorts to yet another attempt at self-verification, this time through his work, which demands considerable travel. Anna, though, turns this information around: "You leave your wife for such long periods? How can you?" (IV, 35). When Anna offers herself to Kate for company during these periods of solitude, Deeley tries his own one-upmanship: "Won't your husband miss you?" (IV, 35). Anna deflects this point as well: "Of course. But he would understand" (IV, 35). The implication is that Anna's husband is more secure in his maleness than is Deeley, who responds by shifting to a different attempt at promotion: "My work took me to Sicily. My work concerns itself with life all over, you see in every part of the globe. With people all over the globe" (IV, 36). Despite his bravura, he remains apart. First he his unnerved by Anna's line, "Rather beguiling so" (IV, 37), to which Deeley can only mutter to himself: "What the hell does she mean by that?" (IV, 37). Then Kate inquires about the marble floors of Anna's house, and the exchange about the sun's heat on the soles of Anna's feet suggests an intimacy between the women that Deeley, clearly the "odd man out," attempts to shatter with a bizarre image:

I had a great crew in Sicily. A marvellous cameraman. Irving Shultz. Best in the business. We took a pretty austere look at the women in black. The little old women in black. I wrote the film and directed it. My name is Orson Welles.   (IV, 38)

Deeley's last four words are also the closing line to Welles's narration over the ending to *The Magnificent Ambersons*, the second film directed by Welles and a portrait of decaying lives and the fall of one family in particular. A. R. Braunmuller explains further about how the invocation of the director in this play is telling:

> Narration means power. Directing or writing the past means a habitable present. Were Deeley and Anna to have control over their lives which Welles had over the lives of the Ambersons, they could survive, even excel. The play makes the film's nostalgia ashes; the past, impossibly, proves worse than the present, and the present reels out of control as a film never could. (Braunmuller, "A World of Words," 67)

Deeley's wit earns no direct retort. Instead the women talk to themselves, isolating him. Anna virtually offers to take Deeley's place: "Don't let's go out tonight, don't let's go anywhere tonight, let's stay in. I'll cook something, you can wash you hair, you can relax, we'll put on some records" (IV, 39). Kate at first demurs, but before long she allows Anna to choose her outfit for the next day.

Deeley's alienation from these plans recalls Pinter's *A Slight Ache* and Edward's panic in the presence of the invading matchseller. When the fundamental values of Deeley's life are treated as irrelevant, he becomes more anxious to assert himself. At the end of act 1, though, his position becomes untenable, as Anna and Kate plan like a couple settling into domestic bliss. Still, Kate does not join entirely, for she does not want Anna to invite anyone else over, nor does she accept Anna's offer to run Kate's bath. She then exits, leaving Anna and Deeley to stare at each other. The suggestion is that Kate is cleansing herself of the influence of one or both of the people who pursue her.

At the beginning of act 2 the setting is altered significantly, for the pieces of furniture are in the same relation to one another but in reversed position, a switch meant to reflect the intrusive presence of Anna. As the scene opens, she and Deeley are alone, and he begins a new campaign by recalling her past, specifically the bohemian company in whose midst he observed her at the Wayfarers Tavern: "Yes, a whole crowd of them, poets, stunt men, jockeys, standup comedians, that kind of setup. You used to wear a scarf, that's right, a black scarf, and a black sweater, and a skirt" (IV, 45). With such detail he intends to characterize her, thereby limiting her imaginative memory and powers of self-definition. As Deeley says: "It's the truth. I remember clearly" (IV, 46).

Anna comically puts him off. After his supply of detail, she queries: "You're saying we've met before?" (IV, 46). Deeley continues to exert pressure, as he describes Anna's appearance, then announces: "I simply sat sipping my light ale and gazed . . . gazed up your skirt. You didn't object, you found my gaze acceptable" (47). He goes on about her thighs, the same ones he sees now. The assertion is a further attempt to evince his masculine appeal to which, he implies, she was susceptible. Yet even in his memory all he can do is stare, like a voyeur, and therefore his impotence is more evident. He talks about Anna and a nameless girl, most likely Kate, who joined her. The repulsive figures around him, he insists, made him unable to approach Anna and this anonymous woman, and again his own inaction mocks the aggression he seeks to summon. All he can describe are the imprints of buttocks on the sofa where Anna was sitting (IV, 48).

The conversation returns to Kate and her bath, and Deeley and Anna both try to demonstrate command. Deeley is once again prosaic:

> Really soaps herself all over, and then washes the soap off, sud by sud. Meticulously. She's both thorough and, I must say it, sensuous. Gives herself a comprehensive going over, and apart from everything else she does emerge as clean as a new pin. Don't you think?   (IV, 49)

Anna, however, sees a more ethereal side: "She floats from the bath. Like a dream. Unaware of anyone standing, with her towel, waiting for her, waiting to wrap it around her. Quite absorbed" (IV, 50). These reflections reinforce Deeley's crudity, especially in contrast to the more delicate desires Anna manifests. Even when Deeley tries to make Kate sound childlike and helpless, his tone is rough: "Of course, she's totally incompetent at drying herself properly, did you find that? [. . .] You'll always find a few odd unexpected unwanted cheeky globules dripping about" (IV, 50). The increasing brusqueness of Deeley's descriptions of drying clarifies that he knows that Anna's feelings for Kate are more than he can have, or for that matter, more than any man can possess: "Listen, I'll tell you what. I'll do it. I'll do the whole lot. The towel and the powder. After all, I am her husband. But you can supervise the whole thing. And give me some hot tips while you're at it. That'll kill two birds with one stone" (IV, 52). The image of the two of them drying Kate is comic, yet sinister: "But take the competitive spirit beyond the game of wit and behind it lurks a vivid and somewhat frightening image of the very possessiveness that is at the heart of the play . . . " (Martineau, 295).

When Deeley mutters "Christ" (IV, 53), he is articulating disgust with himself, and what follows is an even coarser attempt to disparage Anna. First he refers to her age, then dismisses her from his memory: "If I walked into the Wayfarers Tavern now, and saw you sitting in the corner, I wouldn't recognize you" (IV, 53). The logical inconsistency reflects Deeley's panic, as he is reduced to mindless insult. He knows that in the struggle for power and possession of territory he is being supplanted.

When Kate enters from her bath, Deeley and Anna each court her with lyrics from the Gershwins' "They Can't Take That Away from Me." Kate's silence reminds us, however, that as the object of interest she retains control. In her first speech she criticizes both the city and the country (IV, 55), and the blanket denunciation is Kate's way of expressing independence from both Deeley and Anna.

Even as Kate keeps both Anna and Deeley at a distance, the two remain embattled over possession of her. Anna speaks invitingly of London: "You can have a nice room and a nice gas fire and a warm dressing gown and a nice hot drink, all waiting for you for when you come in" (IV, 55). Kate's reply reflects her lack of interest: "Is it raining?" (IV, 55). Anna virtually begs to fix the hem of Kate's black dress, but Kate remains noncommittal, as she does when Deeley inquires about her drying procedures. He also comments about her smile, and when Anna proclaims innocence, Deeley pursues the topic: "You're not. Not like you were a moment ago, not like you did then. (*To Anna.*) You know the smile I'm talking about?" (IV, 57). Toby Silverman Zinman has suggested that these lines are an echo from the Rodgers and Hart song "Where or When," whose title, also the closing words for each verse, would be an appropriate motif for a play about the uncertainty of the past, as well as a work dominated by so many musical references (Zinman, 56–57).

What may be considered the final movement of the play begins when Anna questions Kate about men from her past: McCabe, Duncan, and Christy. Kate is particularly interested in Christy: "He's so gentle, isn't he? And his humour. Hasn't he got a lovely sense of humor? And I think he's . . . so sensitive. Why don't you ask him round?" (IV, 59). Kate emphasizes qualities in Christy that distinguish him from Deeley, who demonstrates neither humor nor sensitivity. Thus Anna's inquiries may be seen as an oblique attack on Deeley, intended to make Kate dissatisfied with him and, given the absence of the others, to turn to Anna for sympathy.

Deeley's inquiries about Kate's plans are a weak attempt to deflect Anna, for her assault continues with a series of daunting revelations. Anna knew Kate long before Deeley did and thus knows nuances of Kate's early behavior, as well as the fact that she was a parson's daughter. As the memories grow more intimate, the most stinging bit of recollection, whether true or not, is that Anna once stole Kate's underwear to wear at a party: "But I told her that in fact I had been punished for my sin, for a man at the party had spent the whole evening looking up my skirt" (IV, 61). The detail recalls Deeley's earlier story, so that he is now objectified in narrative and weakened further. Anna continues that Kate subsequently encouraged such borrowing when Anna was going out and in fact wanted to hear details of Anna's experiences:

> I would come in late and find her reading under the lamp, and begin to tell her, but she would say no, turn off the light, and I would tell her in the dark. She preferred to be told in the dark. But of course it was never completely dark, what with the light from the gasfire or the light through the curtains, and what she didn't know was that, knowing her preference, I would choose a position in the room from which I could see her face, although she could not see mine. She could hear my voice only. And so she listened and I watched her listen. (IV, 61–62)

The passage is one of the crucial speeches in the play. Anna implies first that she and Kate were so close as to share not only clothes but experiences, a sensation Kate can never share with Deeley. Second, the word "dark" recalls the first word of the play, and for Deeley, as for the audience, now takes on an entirely different meaning: that of an aura of memory upon which Kate drew when thinking of Anna. Once more Deeley is left out. The speech concludes with Anna's description of her voice speaking for both women: hence as a woman she has the capacity to invade Kate's consciousness to an extent that will always be beyond Deeley.

Deeley's reply is the initial step toward capitulation: "Sounds a perfect marriage" (IV, 62). What intimidates him most is the sexual intimacy between the women; thus his only remaining tactic is to become more abusive: "You feel it's my province? Well, you're damn right. It is my province. I'm glad someone's showing a bit of taste at last. Of course it's my bloody province. I'm her husband" (IV, 62). His claim is feeble. After he announces that he finds the entire matter "distasteful" (IV, 62), he blusters again about Anna's husband and his own worldly status. Kate interrupts with a devastating offer: "If you don't like it go" (IV, 63).

Anna realizes that the dismissal is a rejection of Deeley, so she retreats gracefully: "You are welcome to come to Sicily at any time, both of you, and be my guests" (IV, 64). The gesture may be seen as an offer made by one who thinks she is victorious, especially after Anna denies any competition by explaining her reason for coming: "To celebrate a very old and treasured friendship, something that was forged between us long before you knew of our existence" (IV, 64). Despite Anna's claim to be uninterested in competing, the insistence that she knew Kate first maintains the battle.

Nevertheless, triumph eludes Anna. First Deeley takes revenge for his own defeat, claiming that he knew Anna long ago in the Wayfarers Tavern. His ugly memory of her allowing him to look up her dress (IV, 65) crushes the image of artistic sensibility that Anna has cultivated. Thereafter Kate's questions to Deeley confirm that she believes Anna was never so devoted to Kate. Whether Deeley's story is the truth is not important. What matters is that Kate accepts it as truth and in doing so casts doubt on Anna's purity. Deeley virtually admits that his story is false: "If it was her skirt. If it was her" (IV, 67). Anna fights back by accepting it: "Oh, it was my skirt. It was me. I remember your look . . . very well. I remember you well" (IV, 67).

The final blows are delivered by Kate, who belittles Anna: "I remember you lying dead. You didn't know I was watching you. I leaned over you. Your face was dirty" (IV, 67). Anna has always spoken of herself as watching Kate. Now Kate shows that in fact she was in control. The reference to Anna's being dirty, especially coming from Kate, who makes a fetish of cleanliness, suggests utter distaste. Images of dirt and disgust follow, until Kate reaches a climax: "I felt the time and season appropriate and that by dying alone and dirty you had acted with proper decorum. It was time for my bath" (IV, 68). Kate's bath is here a self-purification after the soil Anna has brought to her life. Then Kate turns to Deeley and describes her sexual encounter with him as equally disagreeable: "To grind noses together, in or on" (IV, 68). Deeley had expectations "because he was a man" (IV, 68), but all Kate did was smear his face with dirt (IV, 69). She concludes with a dismissal of both: "Neither mattered. (*Pause.*) He asked me once, at about that time, who had slept in that bed before him. I told him no one. No one at all" (IV, 69). Kate's revelation leaves both combatants, Anna and Deeley, helpless. Deeley sobs, then goes to Kate to lie across her lap, a plea for maternal comfort. When she fails to respond, he is rebuffed and feebly retreats to his chair: alone, without identity, without home. Anna, too, suffers such isolation, for her desire to attach herself to Kate and thereby find emotional sustenance has been rejected.

The final moments are intensified in a very bright light, a contrast to the opening shadows of the play and its very first word: "Dark" (IV, 3). Now, however, some of the uncertainty has been resolved, for Kate has assumed power. Her victory, though, is not the expulsion of the two from her life. Rather it is control of them, as Arthur Ganz notes in comparing Kate with Ruth in *The Homecoming*:

> As the desired sexual object she, like Ruth, has power over those who desire her, though Ruth's power lies in the promise of sexuality, Kate's in the denial. Kate, has, in fact, the power to kill, that is to refuse herself to those who desire her and thus to deny the life they would have through possession of her.
>
> (Ganz, "Mixing Memory and Desire," 175)

Like Ruth, like Flora in *A Slight Ache*, like Stella in *The Collection*, Kate seizes on the need for love and uses that weakness as a basis for power:

> Hence, Kate the silent is the strongest of the three, for she lives alone and self-sufficient in a private world to which neither husband or friend is admitted any farther than the periphery. And because they had seen themselves as central to her life, she—not they—finally has the power both to create and destroy.
> (Kreps, 55)

Throughout Pinter's oeuvre characters who need emotional support inevitably suffer because of that need. In *Old Times* the two victims attempt to bolster themselves through images and stories from the past. Memory and, more important, the creation of memory become their weapon. Their desperation, however, undoes them. Kate's strength is her absence of weakness. She creates narrative that dominates the narratives of the other two, and that mastery ensures personal domination. She finds her purpose, her self-definition, through control of others. Because she feels only what she wants to feel, she can say precisely what she wants to say, and that coldness of mind and emotion is the most powerful weapon of all.

8

Betrayal

The familiar triangle of two men and a woman is the fulcrum of *Betrayal*, Pinter's penultimate full-length play. Yet here the subject is handled in a manner that distinguishes this work from Pinter's other plays, for, as Martin Esslin has noted, we find little comedy of menace, little mystery of background or motivation, and little sense of allegorical overtone (Esslin, *Pinter the Playwright*, 205). The reason for the seeming innocuousness of so much of what happens rests particularly with one dramatic element: language. The characters in *Betrayal* speak with a flatness virtually unique in the Pinter canon. Rarely does any character offer a speech of more than a sentence or two, and none offers poetic eloquence. Yet this blandness, which is at points very funny, is essential to the impact of the play, for the characters themselves lack poetry. The three main figures are rich, successful, and intellectual, but their lives are cold and their emotions blunted. The characters seek the social and marital superiority that help create security and power, but they proceed without passion, as if by animal instinct. Thus what Pinter dramatizes here are love affairs that are sterile, carried on by characters who, as representatives of an entire class or social stratum, are at least partially objects of satire.

The most intriguing aspect of the play is the plot structure, which is in reverse time. We begin with two scenes in 1977, one each in 1975 and 1974, three in 1973, then one in 1971 and one in 1968. This arrangement might, under different circumstances, evoke a tragic irony, as we could gradually gain insight into the dissolution of love. For instance, David Lean's film *Brief Encounter*, based on the play *Still Life* by Noel Coward, opens at the end of the story, then returns to the beginning, so that throughout the movie we are aware that the two protagonists never find happiness together. In *Betrayal*, however, although the overall effect is ironic, the tone is hardly tragic. At no point do we mourn great loss. Instead we feel a pervasive melancholy in relationships that shift seemingly in desperation, as characters struggle to make their emotions matter. We may also feel a measure of poignancy, for as the play develops and the characters go back in time, they become less aware of what will happen to them, while we gain more knowledge of how they end up.

The opening scene establishes the peculiar tone. Emma and Jerry meet two years after their affair has terminated. At first the dialogue is filled with empty phrases, embodied in Jerry's wry comment: "You remember the form. I ask about your husband, you ask about my wife" (*Betrayal*, IV, 161). Emma plays right along. The emphasis on propriety, on maintaining dignity while denying passion, contributes to the play's satiric edge. So does Emma's line, "Just like old times" (IV, 158). The last two words recall Pinter's earlier play, as if the dramatist were announcing his intention to examine a similar theme from a different perspective.

That edge is maintained as Jerry recalls playing with Emma's daughter Charlotte in the kitchen (IV, 165). "Threw her up" is the way he describes the fun. The phrase has overtones of "vomit," and that Jerry uses it so often mocks both his insensitivity to language, a curious weakness for a literary agent, and any romantic style to which he might aspire. The phrase has another potential meaning that recalls *The Homecoming*, when Max speaks of similar treatment by his father: "Pass me around, pass me from hand to hand. Toss me up in the air. Catch me coming down. I remember my father" (III, 35). Resentment lurks close to the surface when Max speaks, and we can imagine that little Charlotte was equally unhappy with Jerry's handling.

The antiromantic aspect of Jerry is emphasized further when Emma recalls passing the apartment where she and Jerry used to meet (IV, 167). He responds with no warm memories but merely shifts the discussion to Casey, the novelist whom Emma may be seeing: "I nearly said, now look, she may be having the occasional drink with Casey, who cares, but she and I had an affair for seven years and none of you bastards had the faintest idea it was happening" (IV, 169). What moves him most is the idea of his unspoken power over other men. He does not retain warm memories of Emma. Instead he relishes the secret superiority his relationship provided. Now, although he denies any jealousy of Casey, the repeated mention of his name and the recollections of Jerry's helping him suggest otherwise.

Jerry's complacency is upset by two revelations. The first is from Emma, who announces that the previous night she told her husband, Robert, about her affair with Jerry, who is put off by the news, if in a characteristically distant manner: "But he's my oldest friend. I mean, I picked his own daughter up in my own arms and threw her up and caught her, in my kitchen. He watched me do it" (IV, 175). He is bothered not by the potential breakup of the relationship, but by the awkwardness of the entire situation.

The second blow to Jerry comes from Robert in the next scene. Jerry has invited him over, ostensibly to clear the air, but Robert makes the enterprise unnecessary by explaining dryly: "I thought you knew [. . .] That I knew. That I've known for years. I thought you knew that" (IV, 182). Jerry is thrown: "You thought I knew?" (IV, 182). Robert goes on to say that not only did he know, but that Emma "confirmed . . . the facts [. . .] a long time ago" (IV, 183). Now Jerry does not know whom to trust. Even more important to him, he has lost his advantage. Once he imagined himself the deceiver, the seducer of another man's wife. Now he finds himself played for something of a fool, as Robert's serenity intimates that Jerry was not enough of a rival to arouse concern. Robert did not even bother telling Judith, Jerry's wife:

> You don't seem to understand that I don't give a shit about any of this. It's true
> I've hit Emma once or twice. But that wasn't to defend a principle. I wasn't inspired
> to do it from any kind of moral standpoint. I just felt like giving her a good
> bashing. The old itch . . . you understand.   (IV, 185)

The phrase "the old itch" suggests an involuntary response, without emotional or ethical attachment. Robert's tone also implies that Jerry's affair with Emma was nothing more than an "itch," a passionless and therefore insignificant coupling. Jerry's attempt to retaliate, to make himself seem more than a periodic stimulation, is to insinuate about Robert's affairs: "But you betrayed her for years, didn't you?" (IV, 186). Robert is equally casual about these: "Oh, yes" (IV, 186). When Jerry is forced to confess that he didn't know about those escapades, Robert virtually emasculates him: "No, you didn't know very much about anything, really, did you?" (IV, 186). All Jerry can say of Emma is: "We used to like each other" (IV, 187). Robert tops even that weak claim: "We still do" (IV, 187). The conversation then peters out, with rambling comments about Casey, other professional concerns, and Robert's reading Yeats in Torcello. Neither man can summon the anger to respond to the other. They seem to be hiding behind a demeanor of indifference, a parody of masculine stoicism, each denying the other the pleasure of seeing his competitor grow frustrated or angry. They seem to regard themselves as creatures functioning according to instinct. Such is the level of their friendship and, by extension, the manners and values of their class.

Thus far we have seen only the aftermath of the affair between Jerry and Emma, and we wonder whether the years have diminished the feeling involved, or, indeed, whether any deep feelings were ever part of it. Scene 3, set two years earlier, begins to resolve the matter. Jerry and Emma are breaking up, but the tone is set from Jerry's first line: "What do you want to do then?" (IV, 191). Given their schedules and responsibilities, including Emma's work at her gallery, their affair has become an inconvenience, and the apartment has not helped. As Emma says: "The fact is that in the old days we used our imagination and we'd take a night and make an arrangement and go to an hotel" (IV, 195). The surreptitiousness was the most exciting aspect of their lives. Now, with that gone, they have nothing to spark them. Jerry tries to imply that he and Emma might have had a more profound relationship: "There are no children here, so it's not the same kind of home" (IV, 196). But Emma quashes his attempt at glamorizing their trysts: "It was never intended to be the same kind of home. Was it?" (IV, 197). To her their affair was nothing more than biologically satisfying. The flat was "for fucking" (IV, 197), not "for loving" (IV, 197), as Jerry would like to believe. Thus here, too, Jerry is reduced to a functionary, not the conquering male he imagined himself to be. In Emma's words: "Well, there's not much of that left, is there?" (IV, 197). The rest of the scene is all business, the disposal of furniture and keys. It ends with Emma's cold evaluation: "Listen. I think we've made absolutely the right decision" (IV, 200). She dismisses Jerry's attempts to view their affair as more than it was.

Emma's independence is important to the play. "She is wife, mother, lover, and manager of an art gallery. Yet she does not occupy the familiar position that Pinter has assigned to women in other plays. She is not only an object for male conquest..." (Ben-Zvi, 228). Nevertheless, Emma retains what may be regarded as a traditional feminine desire for domesticity. In scenes 6 and 8 (later in the play, but earlier in the story), she attempts to make the relationship with Jerry more familial by cooking for both of them. She also asks whether she and Jerry will ever travel together (IV, 235), but in both scenes Jerry's blundering destroys hopes for the pair to share anything like a home. Here, as in *The Collection*, *Landscape*, and *Silence*, female needs and desires remain unfulfilled.

In scene 4 the irony of Jerry's delusions is presented with greater sharpness. In the first line Robert calls out: "Emma! Jerry's here!" (IV, 201), to which Emma returns: "Who?" (IV, 201). Perhaps she does not hear Robert, or perhaps she is trying to remain nonchalant. In either case, her failure to recognize his name deflates the passion the two supposedly share. The ensuing discussion between Robert and Jerry about girl and boy babies and their comparative reluctance to face the world concludes with Jerry's dumbly innocent question: "Do you think it might have something to do with the difference between the sexes?" (IV, 205). His lack of understanding of this particular issue mirrors the unawareness he has demonstrated about the feelings of Robert and Emma. Such naïveté is further exposed when he asks why Emma does not approve of Casey's most recent novel, a story of marital infidelity. Jerry enjoyed the work, but Emma recognizes it for what it is: "[. . .] bloody dishonest" (IV, 206). She comprehends the underlying nature and consequences of betrayal and is not taken in by a fictional version. Jerry, as usual, is fooled.

The most telling speeches of the scene refer to the squash-playing by the men. Robert reveals that he has been competing regularly with Casey, "a brutally honest squash player" (IV, 208). (How often these characters invoke some form of the word "honest," a trenchant irony in a play in which deception of all kinds pervades.) That Jerry no longer participates implies that he is failing to uphold the responsibilities of male friendship, which in some respects is a greater betrayal than his affair with Emma. Soon Robert reflects at length on the squash game and explains why Emma would not be welcome:

> Well, to be brutally honest, we wouldn't actually want a woman around, would we, Jerry? I mean a game of squash isn't simply a game of squash, it's rather more than that. You see, first there's the game. And then there's the shower. And then

there's the pint. And then there's lunch. After all, you've been at it. You've had your battle. What you want is your pint and your lunch. You really don't want a woman buying lunch. You don't actually want a woman within a mile of the place, any of the places, really. You don't want her on the squash court, you don't want her in the shower, pub, or the restaurant [. . .].   (IV, 209–210)

The reference to the shower and the use of the phrase "you've been at it" have homoerotic overtones. The speech more strongly implies the elemental competition of two men fighting for survival, as two male primates might battle for leadership of a pack. The reason Emma is not welcome is twofold: one, the struggle is one of male initiation; two, she is the unspoken prize for the winner. Just as the most desirable females in an animal tribe are often rewards for the supreme male, so, Robert implies, is Emma the prize sought by the two men. Thus the satisfaction of victory is not to be taken to lunch by Emma, but to return to Emma and "take" her.

When we put this speech in the context of earlier scenes, in which we were made aware that at this moment Robert knows of the affair between Jerry and Emma, we realize that Robert is putting to Jerry a most basic challenge. Jerry demurs: "I haven't played squash for years" (IV, 210). He does not challenge Robert for Emma. Instead he backs away, surrendering her. Therefore at the end of the scene Emma breaks down and cries in Robert's arms. The passion she may have had for Jerry has been dispelled, at least partially. That she seeks comfort from Robert implies that however fragile their relationship might be, her feelings about him run deeper than those she has for Jerry.

This sense is undercut by scene 5, set one year earlier, which reveals more of the marriage between Emma and Robert. In particular, it shows the antagonism between the two. At the beginning they speak of imminent plans, and the terse lines, though outwardly civil, communicate mutual coolness. Outward tension is manifested only when Robert suggests that he and Emma have lunch with Jerry to discuss a manuscript. The book, ironically, concerns betrayal, about which Robert claims: "Oh . . . not much more to say on that subject, really, is there?" (IV, 216). The atmosphere, however, becomes quickly charged, as Robert muses about the Italian mail service:

So let's say I, whom they laughingly assume to be your husband, had taken the letter, having declared myself to be your husband but in truth being a total stranger, and opened it, and read it, out of nothing more than idle curiosity, and then thrown it in a canal, you would never have received it and would have been deprived of your legal right to open your own mail, and all this because of Venetian je m'en foutisme. I've a good mind to write to the Doge of Venice about it.   (IV, 218)

The last line is an example of a characteristic Pinter technique: the acid joke, seemingly harmless, that masks painful tension. As Robert speaks, we are aware that he very much doubts his place as Emma's husband, and what he perceives as the casual Italian attitude toward marital status mirrors what Robert fears is Emma's insouciance about Robert himself and about the affair with Jerry that Robert is about to bring to light. As Robert adds a few lines later: "What they of course did not know, and had no way of knowing, was that I am your husband" (IV, 218). Robert states this fact as if he were establishing his maleness and laying claim to possessions. When he recounts his school days with Jerry, we feel Robert defending his masculine birthright, the territory he has staked out, namely Emma, against another male invader: "Well, we still are close friends. All that was long before I met you. Long before he met you. I've been trying to remember when I introduced him to you. I simply can't remember. I take it I *did* introduce him to you? Yes. But when? Can you remember?" (IV, 221). His dwelling on trivia masks his anger, a strategy he invokes moments later when Emma declares of herself and Jerry: "We're lovers" (IV, 222). Robert does not give the stark statement the dignity of a pause before responding. Instead he answers: "Ah. Yes. I thought it might be something like that, something along those lines" (IV, 222). His casualness derogates any affections Emma and Jerry might muster and hence salvages Robert's own ego. As if in retaliation, Emma further humiliates him by revealing that the affair has been ongoing for five years. His response, *"Five years?"* (IV, 224), rare italicized words in Pinter's texts (Dukore, *Harold Pinter*, 110), may be read as astonishment or fury. He carries his own counterattack one step further by disparaging his relationship with Emma: "I've always liked Jerry. To be honest, I've always liked him rather more than I've liked you. Maybe I should have had an affair with him myself" (IV, 225). Whether this irony is an unintentional confession is unclear. In any case, Robert implies that a bond between males is more important than one between a man and a woman, which is created for the purposes of procreation but means little more:

Neither Robert nor Jerry can forgive Emma for being a woman—the woman as wife, mother, and whore who pervades Pinter's dramatic world. It is as if all the betrayals in the play find their ultimate source in some primal rage that men feel as sons of women who begat them through betraying them with their fathers— hence the continuing competition with the father and the continuing love/hate relationship with the mother. Torn between her men, choosing now the father, now the son, the woman is considered a whore by both men who have cast her in that role from the beginning.   (Burkman, "Harold Pinter's *Betrayal*," 512)

Burkman here articulates a theme that underlies much of Pinter's work. Many of his male characters seem to resent women not for any conscious reason, but out of some unspoken instinct. In *A Slight Ache* Edward desires Flora, but at moments his frustration at the competition he endures for her overflows, as when he shouts: "You lying slut! Get back to your trough!" (I, 193). In *The Lover* Richard pursues Sarah, but no matter which persona he assumes, he manifests resentment by disparaging her appearance. Even though he loves her, he is antagonistic toward her. All the men of *The Homecoming* desire Ruth; yet they also constantly sneer at women and narrate incidents of brutality, as well as turn on one another in the struggle to possess Ruth for themselves. In *The Basement* Stott and Law compete at squash, as Robert and Jerry do. And just as Emma's coolness here mocks the efforts and affections of both men, so does Jane's detachment set Stott and Law more viciously against each other. From the start of *Old Times* Deeley's anger at Kate's divided loyalty is palpable. Throughout Pinter's work, then, instinctual conflicts are fought among men for possession of women as well as between men and women for dominance in relationships.

That Robert's estimation of the fervor between Jerry and Emma is at least partially correct is clear in scene 6, which takes place later in the summer of 1973. The two are at their most passionate, but even on this occasion the relationship seems stale. As they sip wine and talk, Jerry asks about whether Robert and Emma visited Torcello (IV, 228). Here is the moment when she should reveal the truth of the previous scene, inviting full commitment from Jerry and perhaps giving the two of them the chance to break away from their respective marriages. Instead she tells nothing of Robert's awareness, and the conversation dwindles into banalities.

Only when Jerry mentions taking Robert to lunch is Emma stirred, seeking the reason why: "Well, quite simply, you often do meet, or have lunch, to discuss a particular writer or a particular book, don't you? So to those meetings, or lunches, there is a point or a subject" (IV, 232). Perhaps she fears that Robert will reveal to Jerry what she has kept clandestine. Her desire for secrecy is made more dramatic by Jerry's story about misplacing one of Emma's letters. When he concludes that he found it after all, she replies only: "God" (IV, 236). By withholding information Emma clarifies that her feelings for Jerry are not substantial, that he is but a diversion, a relief from Robert and not a source of love in himself.

Scene 7, set later during 1973, unites the tones of anger and comedy. As Robert and Jerry chat over drinks, we know that Robert is aware of the affair between Jerry and Emma but that Jerry is unaware of Robert's knowledge. Thus we are struck by Robert's struggle to promote civility; we are conscious as well that many lines have overtones of which Robert is conscious and Jerry is not. For instance, speaking of squash, Robert remarks: "Oh yes. We really must play. We haven't played for years" (IV, 241). Earlier we understood the game to mean much more than a simple sporting occasion. Here Robert is challenging Jerry, but the actual contest is a fight for Emma.

The underlying implications of the occasion are comically set off by the waiter, who speaks Italian and conducts himself with the utmost formality. The contrast between his punctiliousness and the resentment in the insinuations offered by Robert create a tension that recalls Pinter's earlier plays of menace. So does the bland questioning about travel and family, as each mention of Emma reminds us of what Robert knows and of what Jerry remains unaware. Eventually Robert's inner turmoil explodes in his diatribe against the modern novel, an outburst obviously aimed at what Emma and Jerry share: "You know what you and Emma have in common? You love literature. I mean you love modern prose literature, I mean you love the new novel by the new Casey or Spinks. It gives you both a thrill" (IV, 250). Jerry is nonplussed by this outburst and, as we have seen, never grasps what torments Robert. In fact, even as we are absorbed by Robert's bitterness, we mock Jerry's obliviousness, secure in our knowledge that he will remain blind for years.

In scene 8 Jerry becomes even more foolish. We see him and Emma at what should be a rapturous moment, an early stage of their affair, but they are burdened by petty concerns. First Emma reveals that she met Judith,

Jerry's wife, who was at lunch with an unknown lady. Jerry is immediately on guard, not only about his wife, but also about Emma: "What were you doing at Fortnum and Mason's?" (IV, 257). Throughout the play the numerous references to Jerry's client Casey have subtly implied that Emma may have been having an affair with him even as she was having one with Jerry. We know additionally that Robert has indulged in a variety of affairs, none of which he has regarded seriously. Now Jerry is concerned not only about this unknown woman lunching with his wife (the dialogue implies his worry about a lesbian relationship), but also about another doctor at the hospital: "He takes her for drinks. It's . . . irritating. I mean, she says that's all there is to it. He likes her, she's fond of him, etcetera, etcetera . . . perhaps that's what I find irritating. I don't know exactly what's going on" (IV, 259). Linda Wells puts this last tension into the context of the entire play:

> Like Emma and Robert, Jerry seeks both the knowledge from others which gives him power and avoids the disclosure of that knowledge which would empower others to withdraw the love and attention he craves. Thus all of the characters engage in power struggles, they use knowledge to vie for that power and to punish their betrayers, and they display their dependency upon others for ego-reflection.
>
> (Wells, 28)

Finally Emma puts the question directly to Jerry: "Do you think she's being unfaithful to you?" (IV, 260). This query leads to other casual, yet ironic, questions, for the participants are concerned about fidelity in an inherently duplicitous relationship. All their concerns suggest that these wealthy, upper-class intellectuals, engaged in an endless process of hopping joylessly from bed to bed, are propelled by biological urges and unwilling or unable to see the emptiness of their lives. In Martin Esslin's words: "[The sexual relationships] seem casual and trivial, hardly more involving than the occasional drunken binge, a form of amusement that will pass the time and alleviate the boredom of an affluent and meaningless existence" (Esslin, *Pinter the Playwright*, 214).

Their lack of emotional substance is emphasized in the last few lines of this scene. Jerry and Emma tonelessly proclaim affection, when Emma suddenly reveals that she is pregnant: "It wasn't anyone else. It was my husband" (IV, 262). The last sentence implies that Jerry would naturally wonder about another man, and the intimation mocks the affection for Jerry she has claimed. Jerry's torpid response, however, suggests that he is so emotionally deadened as to be either relieved that the child is not his or else unconcerned about any implications she is bothering to deny. Earlier in the scene Emma had asked Jerry: "Tell me . . . have you ever thought . . . of changing your life?" (IV, 259). Now she seems to propose that he would be interested in living with or marrying her: "Though the child is Robert's, Emma could transfer responsibility to Jerry: apparently one man will do as well as another" (Diamond, "Pinter's *Betrayal*," 207). Again, we feel human beings pairing off strictly according to biological drive: without rationality, without affection, without any of the emotional support that we traditionally regard as part of "civilized" behavior.

The final scene, the beginning of the story, as it were, presents the initial statement of infatuation between Emma and Jerry. The latter's declarations of ardor are carried on at length:

> I can't wait for you, I'm bowled over, I'm totally knocked out, you dazzle me, you jewel, my jewel, I can't ever sleep again, no, listen, it's the truth, I won't walk, I'll be a cripple, I'll descend. I'll diminish, into total paralysis, my life is in your hands, that's what you're banishing me to, a state of catatonia [. . .].   (IV, 266)

The overstatement makes Jerry a parody of a Renaissance lover, who, with Petrarchan anguish, pines for his unattainable love. Although Jerry may be conscious of his literary license and revel in the exaggerated claims, we know another irony: that his desire is soon to diminish to a point at which he and Emma are parrying lifelessly about one another's feelings. The claims of friendship between Robert and Jerry, though understated, are equally meaningless.

The play thus ends on the same ironic, if wistful, tone that has pervaded it. The three principals have flitted from bed to bed, acting out of jealousy or a desire for retribution or from motivation even flimsier than that. For all the talk about sex, their lives are particularly unerotic. Emma seems to choose Jerry most of all so that she can revenge Robert's dalliances. Jerry seems to relish the superiority of knowing he has slept with his best friend's wife, while Robert finds power in knowing of Jerry's deception and not bothering to reveal the knowledge. Such are the stakes in the warfare that underlies this mode of life. For all three characters, affairs are a way of providing temporary identity and purpose while avoiding substantial feeling. The characters deny this reality by refusing to look at themselves honestly. As much as they betray others, they also betray themselves. Therefore they are laughable, but the comedy is tempered by our realization of the truth they avoid.

Conclusion

"Mr. Pinter is neither pretentious, pseudo-intellectual, nor self-consciously propagandist . . . He writes with an unmistakable sense of theater" (quoted in Hewes, 96). That early verdict came from what may seem an unlikely source: Noel Coward. On reflection the praise should not surprise us, for Coward's sophisticated comedies and Pinter's comedies of menace have more in common than might initially appear.

The measure of any dramatist is how effectively he or she brings us into a unique dramatic world. Both Coward and Pinter are theatrical stylists, and within a moment after the curtain goes up they transport us. Both playwrights also invoke precise, often elliptical, dialogue that characters use to shield themselves from a reality that offers little in which to believe.

Coward's characters hide behind a mask of lightheartedness: "His frivolity celebrates a metaphysical stalemate, calling it quits with meanings and certainties" (Lahr, 3). For instance, in *Private Lives*, a portrait of love hopelessly, but comically, intermingled with antagonism, Elyot is accused by his ex-wife Amanda, with whom he has just reunited: "You have no faith, that's what wrong with you" (*Private Lives*, 30). He agrees unhesitatingly: "Absolutely none" (*Private Lives*, 30). Moments later Elyot cautions her: "You mustn't be serious, my dear one, it's what they want" (*Private Lives*, 33). In the face of meaninglessness, Coward's characters put up a facade of artifice, and that style becomes their substance. Only rarely do they confront the hollowness of their existence, and even then they jump from the topic as soon as possible. Thus the tone of the plays is almost perpetually buoyant.

Pinter's characters, however, function in a darker environment. The incertitude of their lives, the lack of assurance or reliable belief in any agency, whether social, religious, or political, is never avoided for long. His characters are absorbed with the contention for personal and intellectual dominance, and they disguise their fear in verbiage, but awareness of the tenuousness of existence is never far from their consciousness.

As a result his characters seem perpetually in the midst of a struggle. It is one that is elemental in nature, in which the primary goal is security, often in the form of power: the right to lay claim to a home and to demand sustenance, both physical and emotional. The measure of the happiness of their lives is the quality of this survival.

The battle, however, is not always conducted on polite or even what we might call "civilized" terms. Indeed, it is often brutal, a "survival of the fittest." In an early review of *The Homecoming*, Ronald Bryden called the play Pinter's "funniest, best-constructed, most characteristic, most explicit" (Bryden, 928). He also quotes one theatergoer who said of the play's characters: "They're exactly like animals!" (Bryden, 928), and for Bryden that image is the key to the play. Indeed, his analysis is filled with references to "beasts" and "territory," a theme picked up by other critics. For instance, Arthur Ganz, commenting on *The Homecoming*, writes about "all those blind, brutal, hostile impulses which, sweeping aside the restraints of intellect and morality, make their own fearful claims to be part of any vital existence" (Ganz, "A Clue to the Pinter Puzzle," 187).

A major aspect of this struggle is carried on between men and women, who share certain human necessities, but whose intellectual and emotional composition differs fundamentally, and who therefore compete against one another from disparate perspectives and with disparate weapons. The women in Pinter's plays seem to have greater awareness, both of their own natures and of the nature of men, and this understanding gives women a strength, a capacity for survival, that the male characters lack. At the same time the women have emotional needs that are not fulfilled by possession of space or authority. They participate in the competition for such prizes, but with a different emphasis: ". . . oftentimes the Pinter woman craves dominance as her only means of achieving the psychological wholeness and integration she desires and demands for herself as a person" (Adler, "Notes Toward the Archetypal Pinter Woman," 377).

Furthermore, some of the specific qualities of Pinter's female characters have changed over the course of his career. In earlier plays they are largely reflections of male attitudes, and therefore alternate between the roles of mother, wife, and whore. In later works Pinter dramatizes other aspects of female nature, most importantly a refinement of sensibility. Throughout his works, however, Pinter has always dramatized men and women as contrasting fundamentally. Though both genders compete for power, women have different goals and desires, and Pinter portrays these with sympathy. Sometimes the women triumph on their own terms, and their victory is a reflection of the primitive as well as the refined in human nature.

Since *Betrayal*, Pinter's output for the stage has been small. His few brief works have continued to focus on power, but the emphasis has shifted. Instead of dramatizing the complexities of dominance within individual relationships, especially in regard to the dynamics of gender, Pinter has concentrated on conflicts between the individual and the surrounding political structure. In *Mountain Language* prisoners in an unnamed fascist country are persecuted as they attempt to speak the language that they have always known and that gives them identity. In *One for the Road* individual members of a family are brought before an inquisitor who subjects them to a barrage of questions meant to destroy their will and thus their individuality. In both works the figures of authority are male, and some of the victims are female, but issues of gender are minor. The nature of power is at the core of these plays, but Pinter's concern is clearly political and intellectual oppression.

In *Party Time*, men and women are absorbed in various struggles for dominance, but these are portrayed with deep irony, for the social strategies take place against the background of a city and society under siege. The characters, even more flighty and empty than those from *Betrayal*, bicker and gossip about club facilities, as well as about various affairs, flirtations, and jealousies, all the while ignoring the tragedy surrounding them. This attitude is embodied in one speech by the host, Gavin:

> That's all we ask, that the service this country provides will run on normal, secure, and legitimate paths and that the ordinary citizen be allowed to pursue his

labours and his leisure in peace. Thank you all so much for coming here tonight.
It's been really lovely to see you, quite smashing.   (*Party Time*, 37)

This insouciance may be understood as Pinter's condemnation of what he
sees as the unwillingness of his own society, as well as others, to confront
the realities of political terrorism around the world.

The themes of identity and the search for meaning are the core of *A Kind
of Alaska*, a one-act play inspired by Oliver Sacks's book *Awakenings*. This
clinical study details the cases of victims of encephalitis lethargica ("sleeping
sickness") who with the development of a remarkable drug were brought back
to consciousness. The play's main character, Deborah, returns to life after
thirty years in a catatonic state, left only with images of people and places
long gone or profoundly changed. Pinter effectively dramatizes the memories of adolescent girlhood, the complex network of affection, jealousy, and
doubt. Yet although the protagonist is female, the emphasis of the play is
less on gender than on the transience of human existence and the evanes-
cence of knowledge. Furthermore, the male doctor who cares for Deborah
is a figure of compassion. Despite his marriage to her sister, he has devoted
himself to his patient. The play is thus largely elegiac, and the struggle for
territorial dominance that marks many of Pinter's other works is absent here.

Of Pinter's recent miniatures, one echoes the themes of gender and power:
the enigmatic *Family Voices*, first broadcast on radio in 1981 and one month
later transferred to the stage. The next year it was "read" as part of an evening
of short works collectively titled *Other Places*. In many respects it should be
judged as a coda to one aspect of Pinter's work, and as such it will bring this
book to a close.

The primary speaker is a young man, and the other two voices, that of his
mother and dead father, probably emanate from the young man's mind. From
the outset we intuit a protagonist whose identity is shaken. He has broken
away from home, but the existence of this trio of voices suggests that he can
never escape completely, that the memory and values he has taken with him
bolster a sense of self. That the young man jokes with his mother about
drinking alcohol, then confesses he never touched it (IV, 282), suggests her
domination. Indeed, he seems to have found a substitute for her: Mrs.
Withers, his landlady. In his mind, however, his mother never lets go:
"Darling I miss you. I gave birth to you. Where are you?" (IV, 284).

One member of the household is of particular interest. Her name is Jane, and she is a fifteen-year-old schoolgirl whom the young man describes as sipping tea while her feet rest in the young man's lap and her toes wiggle (IV, 286-287). This description is followed by a cry of loneliness from the mother's voice: "Darling. Where are you? Why do you never write?" (IV, 287). The son is torn between sexual desire and loyalty to his mother, a familiar theme for Pinter. The young man seeks sexual dominance over the girl and his mother, for such power will give him authority in his own life. The mother rants about her own frustrations, and we feel that even if she is a tyrant over her son, her actions must be judged sympathetically. As she says of herself: "Sometimes I think I have always been sitting like this. I sometimes think I have always been sitting like this, alone by an indifferent fire, curtains closed, night, winter" (IV, 289).

At moments the son seems to have found security: "Oh mother, I have found my home, my family. Little did I ever dream I could know such happiness" (IV, 290). But other inhabitants of the house befuddle the young man:

> If either is the case why isn't Jane called Lady Jane Withers? Or perhaps she is. Or perhaps neither is the case? Or perhaps Mrs Withers is actually the Honorable Mrs Withers? But if that is the case what does that make Mr Withers? And which Withers is he anyway? I mean what relation is he to the rest of the Witherses? And who is Riley? (IV, 293)

Here is the fruitless desire for certainty, the vain attempt at verification, that pervades the Pinter canon. The son's desire for power is constantly frustrated.

At last the third voice is heard, denying his own death: "A quick word for old time's sake. Just to keep in touch. An old hullo out of the dark. A last kiss from Dad" (IV, 294). The young man can never entirely leave his family and past. In desperation he tries to retreat:

> I'm coming back to you, mother, to hold you
> in my arms.
>
> I am coming home.
>
> I am coming also to clasp my father's
> shoulder.   (IV, 295)

The sudden ending implies the inevitable isolation of all three characters. Their voices never intersect, their doubts never resolve, their fears never dissolve.

The young man in *Family Voices* grasps what is understood by all of Pinter's characters: the ultimate isolation of the individual human being, trapped in a disjointed world, where cries for help and love echo, then fade. These characters, however, do not surrender in helplessness. They fight back, both consciously and instinctively, with a variety of weapons: sexuality, physicality, language, knowledge, and memory. In response to the void about them, they struggle for security, especially through domination over territory. The focus of this book is how this struggle is common to men and women, shared by them, yet fought in opposition. Sexual drive and a need for love propels men and women toward one another. Other instincts and desires drive them apart. Thus their relationships are necessary and intimate, yet contentious and often painful. One goal remains paramount: power, the capacity to impose will and thereby create order, establish values, and find meaning, purpose, and identity.

Works Cited

Adler, Thomas P. "Notes Toward the Archetypal Pinter Woman." *Theatre Journal* 33, no. 3 (October 1981): 377–85.

———. "Pinter's *Night*: A Stroll down Memory Lane." *Modern Drama* 17 (December 1974): 461–65.

Almansi, Guido, and Simon Henderson. *Harold Pinter*. London: Methuen and Co., 1983.

Ardrey, Robert. *The Territorial Imperative*. New York: Dell, Publishing Co., 1966.

Bardwick, Judith. *Psychology of Women*. New York: Harper and Row, 1971.

Beckett, Samuel. *Krapp's Last Tape and Other Dramatic Pieces*. New York: Grove Press, 1960.

———. *Waiting for Godot*. New York: Grove Press, 1954.

Ben-Zvi, Linda. "Harold Pinter's *Betrayal*: The Patterns of Banality." *Modern Drama* 23 (September 1980): 227–37.

Bernhard, F. J. "Beyond Realism: The Plays of Harold Pinter." *Modern Drama* 8 (September 1965): 185–91.

Braunmuller, A.R. "Pinter's *Silence*: Experience Without Character." In *Harold Pinter: Critical Approaches*, edited by Steven H. Gale. Rutherford, N.J.: Fairleigh Dickinson University Press, 1986.

———. "A World of Words in Pinter's *Old Times*." *Modern Language Quarterly* 40, no. 1 (March 1979): 53–74.

Brown, John Russell. "*The Homecoming* and Other Plays by Harold Pinter." In *Modern British Dramatists: New Perspectives*, edited by John Russell Brown. Englewood Cliffs, N.J.: Prentice-Hall, 1984.

Bryden, Ronald. "A Stink of Pinter." *New Statesman*, June 1965, 928.

Burghardt, Lorraine Hall. "Game Playing in Three by Pinter." *Modern Drama* 17 (December 1974): 377–88.

Burkman, Katherine M. "Death and the Double in Three Plays by Harold Pinter." In *Harold Pinter: You Never Heard Such Silence*, edited by Alan Bold. London: Vision Press, 1984.

———. *The Dramatic World of Harold Pinter: Its Basis in Ritual*. Columbus, OH: Ohio State University Press, 1971.

———. "Harold Pinter's *Betrayal*: Life Before Death—and After." *Theatre Journal* 34 (December 1982): 505–18.

———. "Pinter's *A Slight Ache* as Ritual." *Modern Drama* 11 (December 1968): 326–35.

Cohn, Ruby. *Currents in Contemporary Drama*. Bloomington, IN: Indiana University Press, 1969.

Coward, Noel. *Private Lives*. New York: Samuel French, 1930.

Diamond, Elin. "Pinter's *Betrayal* and the Comedy of Manners." *Modern Drama* 23 (September 1980): 238–45.

———. *Pinter's Comic Play*. Lewisburg, PA: Bucknell University Press, 1985.

Dukore, Bernard F. *Harold Pinter*. New York: Grove Press, 1982.

———. "What's in a Name?—An Approach to *The Homecoming*." *Theatre Journal* 33 (May 1981): 173–81.

———. *Where Laughter Stops: Pinter's Tragicomedy*. Columbia, MO: University of Missouri Press, 1976.

———. "A Woman's Place." In *A Casebook on Harold Pinter's "The Homecoming,"* edited by John Lahr. New York: Grove Press, 1971.

Dutton, Richard. *Modern Tragicomedy and the British Tradition*. Norman, OK: University of Oklahoma Press, 1986.

Eigo, James. "Pinter's *Landscape*." *Modern Drama* 16 (September 1973): 179–83.

Elsom, John. *Post-War British Theatre*. London: Routledge & Kegan Paul, 1976.

Esslin, Martin. *Pinter: The Playwright*. London: Methuen, 1982. Originally published as *The Peopled Wound: The Plays of Harold Pinter*. London: Methuen, 1970. Revised ed. published as *Pinter: A Study of his Plays*. London: Eyre Methuen, 1973; third ed., 1977.

———. *The Theatre of the Absurd*. 3rd ed. Harmondsworth: Penguin, 1980.

Evans, Gareth Lloyd. *The Language of Modern Drama*. London: J. M. Dent & Sons, 1977.

Gabbard, Lucina Paquet. *The Dream Structure of Pinter's Plays*. Cranbury, NJ: Associated University Presses, 1976.

Gale, Steven H. *Butter's Going Up: A Critical Analysis of Harold Pinter's Work*. Durham, NC: Duke University Press, 1977.

———. "Deadly Mind Games: Harold Pinter's *Old Times*" in *Critical Essays on Harold Pinter*, edited by Steven H. Gale. Boston: G. K. Hall, 1990.

Ganz, Arthur. "A Clue to the Pinter Puzzle: The Triple Self in *The Homecoming*." *Educational Theatre Journal* 21 (May 1969): 180–87.

———. "Mixing Memory and Desire: Pinter's Vision in *Landscape, Silence*, and *Old Times*." In *Pinter: A Collection of Critical Essays*, edited by Arthur Ganz. Englewood Cliffs, NJ: Prentice-Hall, 1972.

Genet, Jean. *Deathwatch*. Translated by Bernard Frechtman. New York: Grove Press, 1954, 1961.

———. *The Maids* Translated by Bernard Frechtman. New York: Grove Press, 1954, 1961.

Gordon, Lois. *Stratagems to Uncover Madness: The Dramas of Harold Pinter*. Columbia, MO: University of Missouri Press, 1969.

Hall, Peter. "Directing Pinter." In *Harold Pinter: You Never Heard Such Silence*, edited by Alan Bold. London: Vision Press, 1984.

Hewes, Henry. "Probing Pinter's Play." Interview with Harold Pinter. *Saturday Review* 50 (8 April 1967): 56–58, 96–97.

Hinchliffe, Arnold. "Mr. Pinter's Belinda." *Modern Drama* 11 (September 1968): 173–79.

Hollis, James R. *Harold Pinter: The Poetics of Silence.* Carbondale, IL: Southern Illinois University Press, 1970.

Hudgins, Christopher C. "*The Basement*: Harold Pinter on BBC-TV." *Modern Drama* 28 (March 1985): 71–82.

Hughes, Alan. "Myth and Memory in *Old Times*." *Modern Drama* 17 (December 1974): 467–76.

Kerr, Walter. Review of *The Homecoming*, by Harold Pinter. *New York Times*, 6 January 1967, 29.

Killinger, John. *World In Collapse: The Vision of Absurd Drama.* New York: Dell Publishing Co., 1971.

Kreps, Barbara. "Time and Harold Pinter's Possible Realities: Art as Life, and Vice Versa." *Modern Drama* 22 (March 1979): 47–60.

Lahr, John. *Coward the Playwright.* New York: Avon, 1982.

Lumley, Frederick. *New Trends in 20th Century Drama.* New York: Oxford University Press, 1956, 4th ed., 1972.

Martineau, Stephen. "Pinter's *Old Times*: The Memory Game." *Modern Drama* 16 (December 1973): 287–97.

Mast, Gerald. "Pinter's *Homecoming*." *Drama Survey* 6 (Spring 1968): 266–77.

Moir, Anne, and David Jessel. *Brain Sex.* New York: Carol Publishing Group, 1991.

Nelson, Hugh. "*The Homecoming*: Kith and Kin." In *Modern British Dramatists*, edited by John Russell Brown. Englewood Cliffs, NJ: Prentice-Hall, 1968.

Osherow, Anita R. "Mother and Whore: The Role of Woman in *The Homecoming*." *Modern Drama* 17 (December 1974): 423–32.

Pinter, Harold. *Complete Works*, vols. 1–4. New York: Grove Weidenfeld, 1976, 1977, 1978, 1981.

———. *The Hotbouse*. New York: Grove Press, 1980.

———. *Party Time*. London: Faber and Faber, 1991.

———. "Writing for the Theatre." In Harold Pinter: *Complete Works*, vol. 1. New York: Grove Weidenfeld, 1976.

Pirandello, Luigi. *Naked Masks*. New York: Dutton, 1952.

Postlewait, Thomas. "Pinter's *The Homecoming*: Displacing and Repeating Ibsen." *Comparative Drama* 15 (Fall 1981): 195–212.

Quigley, Austin, E. *The Pinter Problem*. Princeton: Princeton University Press, 1975.

Roberts, Patrick. *The Psychology of Tragic Drama*. London: Routledge & Kegan Paul, 1975.

Rosador, Kurt Tetzeli v. "Pinter's Dramatic Method: *Kullus, The Examination, The Basement*." *Modern Drama* 14 (September 1971): 195–204.

Sakellaridou, Elizabeth. *Pinter's Female Portraits*. Totowa, NJ: Barnes & Noble Books, 1988.

Sarbin, Deborah A. "'I Decided She Was': Representation of Women in *The Homecoming*." *The Pinter Review* 3 (1989): 34–42.

Schechner, Richard. "Puzzling Pinter." *Tulane Drama Review* 11 (Winter 1966): 176–84.

Strindberg, August. *Five Plays*. Translated by Harry Carlson. New York: Signet, 1981, 1983.

Sykes, Alrene. *Harold Pinter*. St. Lucia: University of Queensland Press, 1970.

Taylor, John Russell. *Anger and After*. Harmondsworth: Penguin, 1963.

———. "Pinter's Game of Happy Families." In *A Casebook on Harold Pinter's "The Homecoming*," edited by John Lahr. New York: Grove Press, 1971.

Trussler, Simon. *The Plays of Harold Pinter*. London: Victor Gollancz, 1974.

Wardle, Irving. "The Territorial Struggle." In *A Casebook on Harold Pinter's "The Homecoming*," edited by John Lahr. New York: Grove Press, 1971.

Warner, John M. "The Epistemological Quest in Pinter's *The Homecoming*." *Contemporary Literature* 11 (Summer 1970): 340–53.

Wells, Linda S. "A Discourse on Failed Love: Harold Pinter's *Betrayal*." *Modern Language Studies* 13 (Winter 1983): 22–30.

Wellwarth, George. *The Theater of Protest and Paradox*, revised edition. New York: New York University Press, 1971.

Zinman, Toby Silverman. "Pinter's *Old Times*." *Explicator* 43 (Winter 1985): 56–57.

INDEX

ABOUT THE AUTHOR

Victor L. Cahn is Associate Professor of English at Skidmore College, where he teaches courses in modern drama and in Shakespeare. He has written several plays and four other books, including *Beyond Absurdity: The Plays of Tom Stoppard* and *Shakespeare the Playwright*. His articles and reviews have appeared in such publications as *Modern Drama, The Literary Review, The New York Times,* and *Variety*.